# The Essential Acoustic
# RORY GALLAGHER

GUITAR TAB EDITION

Published by
Hal Leonard

Exclusive distributors:
Hal Leonard
7777 West Bluemound Road,
Milwaukee, WI 53213
Email: info@halleonard.com

Hal Leonard Europe Limited
42 Wigmore Street, Marylebone,
London W1U 2 RY
Email: info@halleonardeurope.com

Hal Leonard Australia Pty. Ltd.
4 Lentara Court, Cheltenham,
Victoria 9132, Australia
Email: info@halleonard.com.au

Order No. AM1005609
ISBN 978-1-78038-763-5

Edited by Adrian Hopkins.
Music arranged by Arthur Dick.
Music engraved by Paul Ewers Music Design.
All images courtesy of Strange Music Limited.
Back cover image: Rory Gallagher mural by
The Bogside Artists in Ballyshannon, Ireland.
Front cover design by Mark Jessett.

Printed in the EU.

www.halleonard.com

Special thanks to Daniel Gallagher for his assistance
in preparing this volume and to Martin Dubka for his help
with proof-reading the arrangements.

Also available:
The Essential Rory Gallagher Vol. 1
Order No. AM992266
The Essential Rory Gallagher Vol. 2
Order No. AM997722
The Essential Rory Gallagher: The Complete Taste Order
No. AM1000395
Play Guitar With Rory Gallagher
Order No. AM1003046

The following additional titles are available
to download from sheetmusicdirect.com:

Cradle Rock
Out On The Western Plain
Overnight Bag
Slumming Angel

## FOREWORD

Rory Gallagher was a genuinely lovely human being for whom music was much more than simply a release — it was a continuing source of wonder: his passion was apparent the moment he started to play and sing. Those who came to know him came quickly to understand that here was an extraordinarily open-minded man who was only ever truly bewildered by anyone else's reluctance to embrace such a notion. I have said before that grace is a word which most especially applies to Rory and that still holds true. My own memories of the man start with that, and as this postscript shows, (thank you Rilke), the song continues sweet.

*Martin Carthy, August 2012*

*No, my life is not this precipitous hour*
*through which you see me passing at a run.*
*I stand before my background like a tree.*
*Of all my many mouths I am but one,*
*and that which soonest chooses to be dumb.*
*I am the rest between two notes*
*which, struck together, sound discordantly,*
*because death's note would claim a higher key.*
*But in the dark pause, trembling, the notes meet,*
*harmonious.*
*And the song continues sweet.*

*from Poems From The Book Of Hours*
*Rainer Maria Rilke*

# GUITAR TABLATURE EXPLAINED

Guitar music can be notated in three different ways: on a musical stave, in tablature, and in rhythm slashes

RHYTHM SLASHES: are written above the stave. Strum chords in the rhythm indicated. Round noteheads indicate single notes.

THE MUSICAL STAVE: shows pitches and rhythms and is divided by lines into bars. Pitches are named after the first seven letters of the alphabet.

TABLATURE: graphically represents the guitar fingerboard. Each horizontal line represents a string, and each number represents a fret.

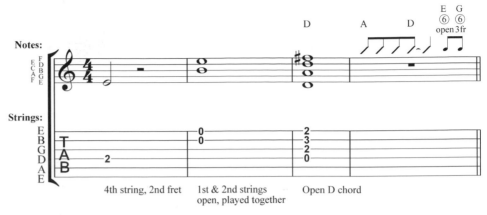

4th string, 2nd fret    1st & 2nd strings open, played together    Open D chord

## Definitions for special guitar notation

**SEMI-TONE BEND:** Strike the note and bend up a semi-tone (½ step).

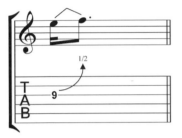

**WHOLE-TONE BEND:** Strike the note and bend up a whole-tone (full step).

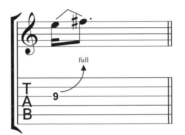

**GRACE NOTE BEND:** Strike the note and bend as indicated. Play the first note as quickly as possible.

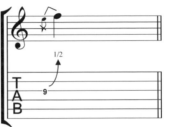

**QUARTER-TONE BEND:** Strike the note and bend up a ¼ step

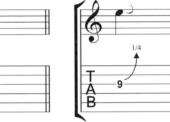

**BEND & RELEASE:** Strike the note and bend up as indicated, then release back to the original note.

**COMPOUND BEND & RELEASE:** Strike the note and bend up and down in the rhythm indicated.

**PRE-BEND:** Bend the note as indicated, then strike it.

**PRE-BEND & RELEASE:** Bend the note as indicated. Strike it and release the note back to the original pitch.

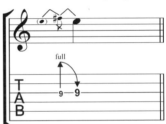

**HAMMER-ON:** Strike the first note with one finger, then sound the second note (on the same string) with another finger by fretting it without picking.

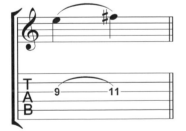

**PULL-OFF:** Place both fingers on the note to be sounded, strike the first note and without picking, pull the finger off to sound the second note.

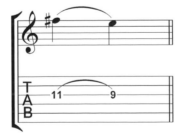

**LEGATO SLIDE (GLISS):** Strike the first note and then slide the same fret-hand finger up or down to the second note. The second note is not struck.

**MUFFLED STRINGS:** A percussive sound is produced by laying the first hand across the string(s) without depressing, and striking them with the pick hand.

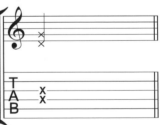

**NATURAL HARMONIC:** Strike the note while the fret-hand lightly touches the string directly over the fret indicated.

**PICK SCRAPE:** The edge of the pick is rubbed down (or up) the string, producing a scratchy sound.

**PALM MUTING:** The note is partially muted by the pick hand lightly touching the string(s) just before the bridge.

**SHIFT SLIDE (GLISS & RESTRIKE** Same as legato slide, except the second note is struck.

**TAP HARMONIC:** The note is fretted normally and a harmonic is produced by tapping or slapping the fret indicated in brackets (which will be twelve frets higher than the fretted note.)

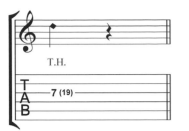

**TAPPING:** Hammer ('tap') the fret indicated with the pick-hand index or middle finger and pull-off to the note fretted by the fret hand.

**PINCH HARMONIC:** The note is fretted normally and a harmonic is produced by adding the edge of the thumb or the tip of the index finger of the pick hand to the normal pick attack.

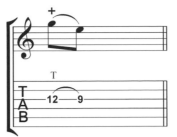

**ARTIFICIAL HARMONIC:** The note fretted normally and a harmonic is produced by gently resting the pick hand's index finger directly above the indicated fret (in brackets) while plucking the appropriate string.

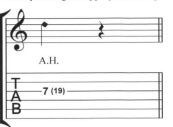

**TRILL:** Very rapidly alternate between the notes indicated by continuously hammering-on and pulling-off.

**RAKE:** Drag the pick across the strings with a single motion.

**TREMOLO PICKING:** The note is picked as rapidly and continously as possible.

**ARPEGGIATE:** Play the notes of the chord indicated by quickly rolling them from bottom to top.

**SWEEP PICKING:** Rhythmic downstroke and/or upstroke motion across the strings.

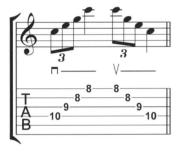

**VIBRATO DIVE BAR AND RETURN:** The pitch of the note or chord is dropped a specific number of steps (in rhythm) then returned to the original pitch.

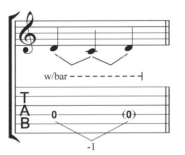

**VIBRATO BAR SCOOP:** Depress the bar just before striking the note, then quickly release the bar.

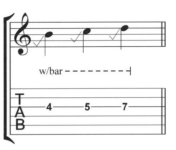

**VIBRATO BAR DIP:** Strike the note and then immediately drop a specific number of steps, then release back to the original pitch.

# Additional musical definitions

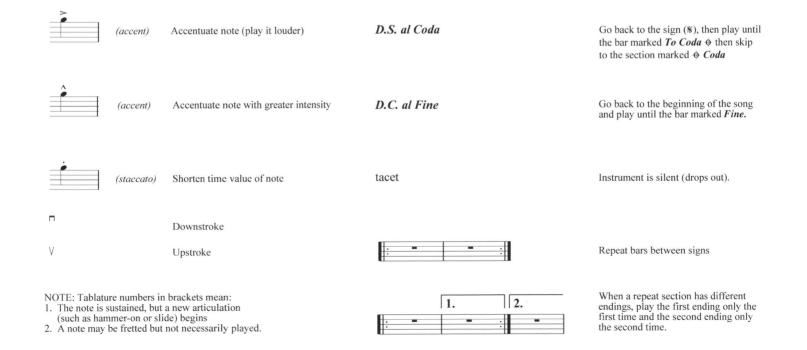

(accent)   Accentuate note (play it louder)

(accent)   Accentuate note with greater intensity

(staccato)   Shorten time value of note

⊓   Downstroke

V   Upstroke

**D.S. al Coda**   Go back to the sign (%), then play until the bar marked **To Coda** ⊕ then skip to the section marked ⊕ **Coda**

**D.C. al Fine**   Go back to the beginning of the song and play until the bar marked **Fine.**

tacet   Instrument is silent (drops out).

Repeat bars between signs

NOTE: Tablature numbers in brackets mean:
1. The note is sustained, but a new articulation (such as hammer-on or slide) begins
2. A note may be fretted but not necessarily played.

When a repeat section has different endings, play the first ending only the first time and the second ending only the second time.

# AS THE CROW FLIES (LIVE)

Words & Music by Tony Joe White

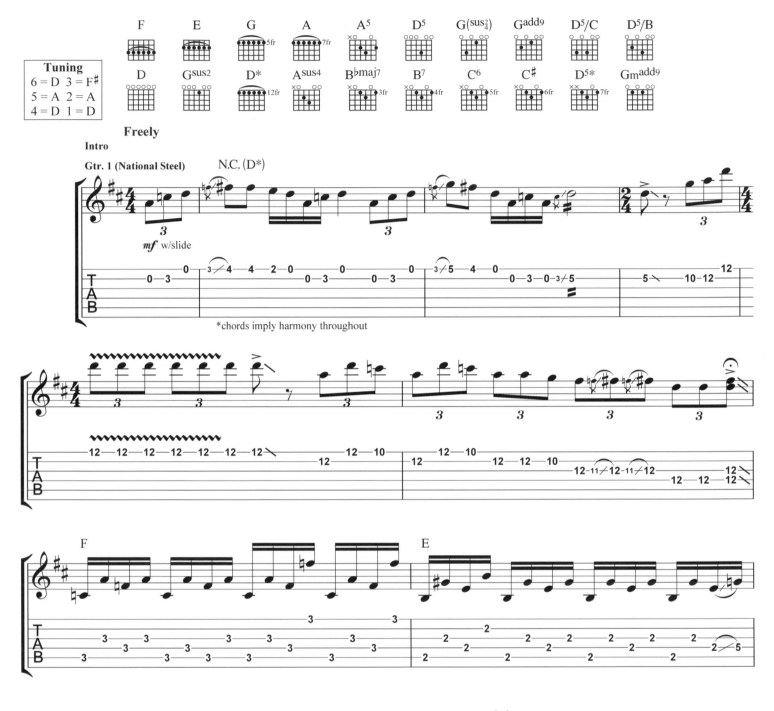

*chords imply harmony throughout

ah ah ah ah ah ah ah ah ah. Ah ah ah ah ah ah ah ah ah ah.__

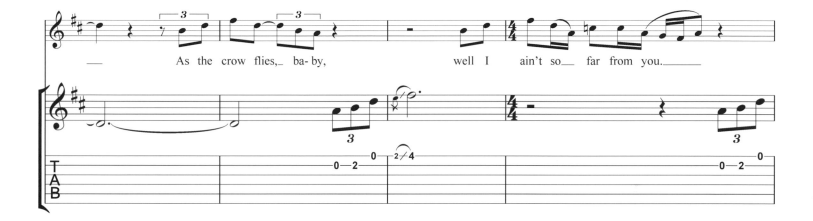

__ As the crow flies,_ ba - by, well I ain't so__ far from you._____

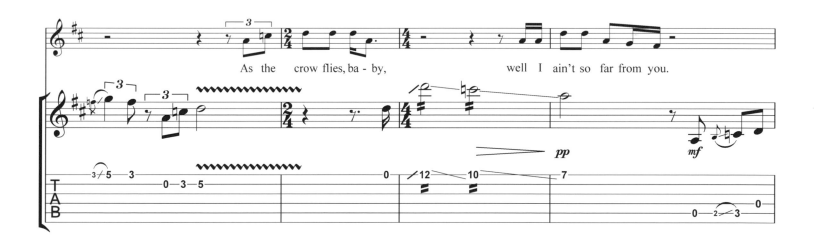

As the crow flies, ba - by, well I ain't so far from you.

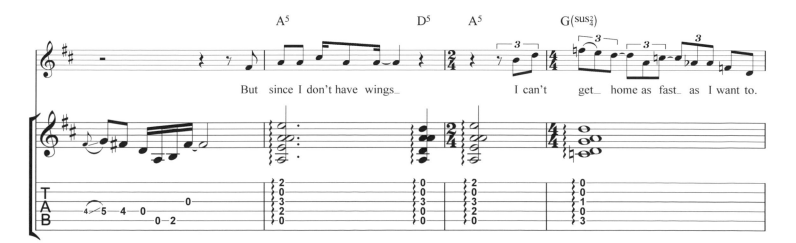

But since I don't have wings__ I can't get__ home as fast_ as I want to.

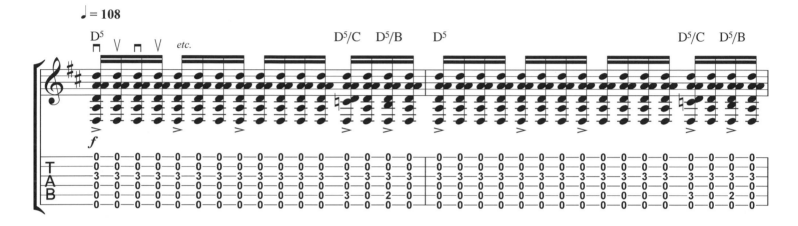

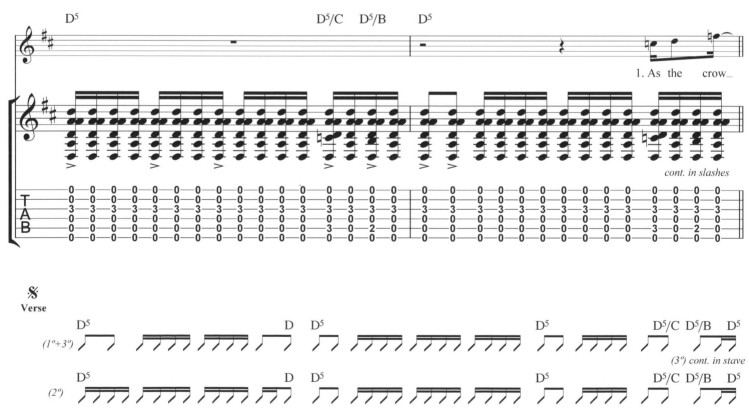

1. As the crow

_flies, babe,          well I     ain't so    far__ from  you.__
last    night,          well I     heard_____  you call my  name.
know   ba-by,          how I    miss  your  sweet_____  ca-ress.

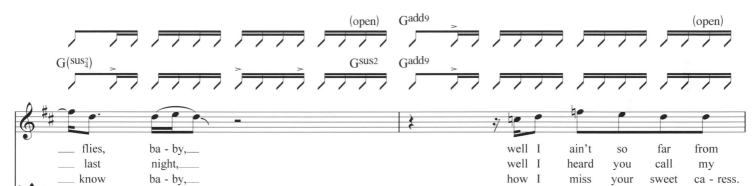

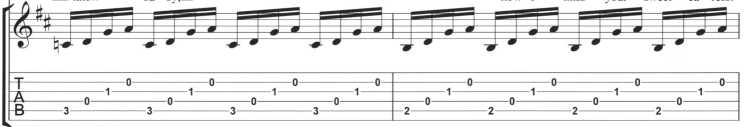

since I don't have wings_____ I can't
took it as an o - men and I
When I'm in your lov - in' arms I

get_____ home as fast as I want__ to._____ Yeah, yeah.
jumped__ on a ver - y fast freight train.
swear I'm at my ver - y best.

As the crow flies.

2. In a dream__

Solo (D)

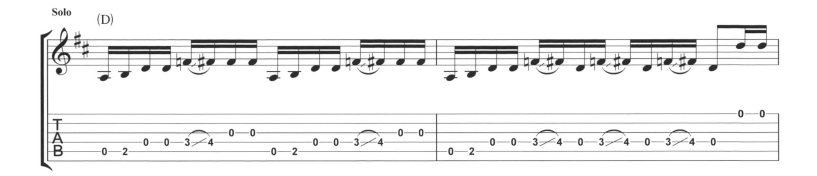

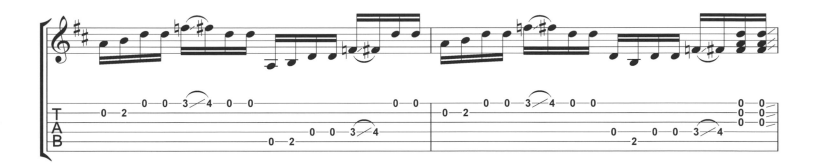

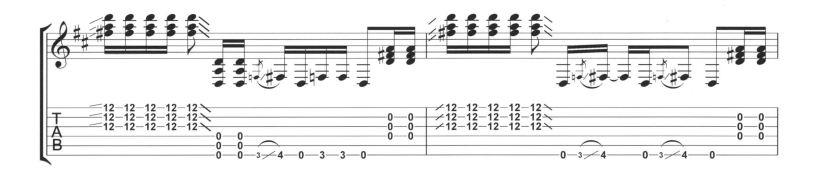

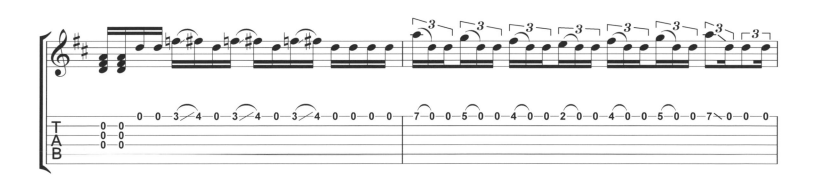

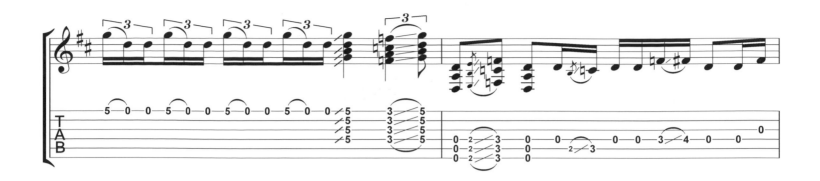

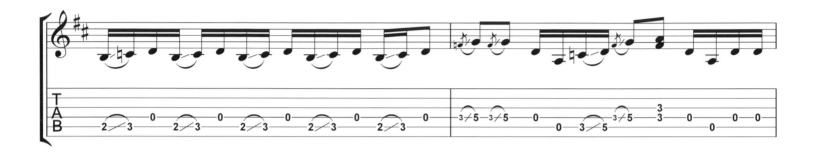

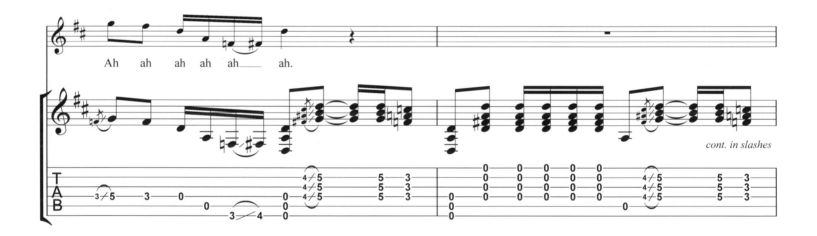

Ah ah ah ah ah___ ah.

*cont. in slashes*

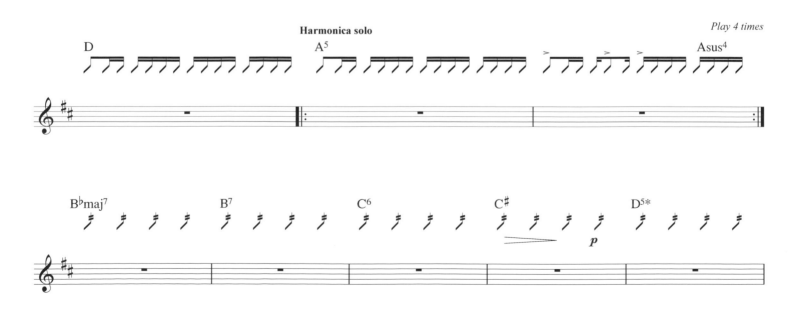

**Harmonica solo**

*Play 4 times*

D          A⁵                    Asus⁴

B♭maj⁷     B⁷        C⁶        C♯        D⁵*

*p*

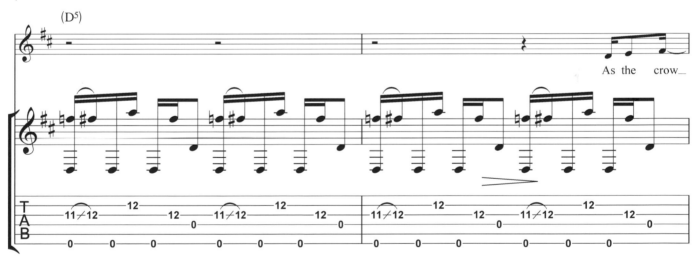

3. Well you don't___

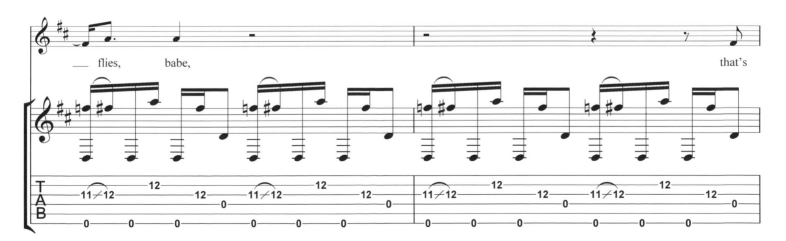

___ flies,      babe,                                                                                    that's

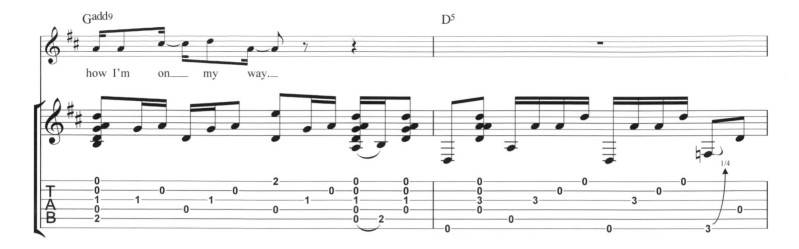

how I'm on— my way.—

As the crow— flies ba - by,—

I'm on my way.— Ah ah ah ah ah ah ah ah ah ah.

*cont. in slashes*

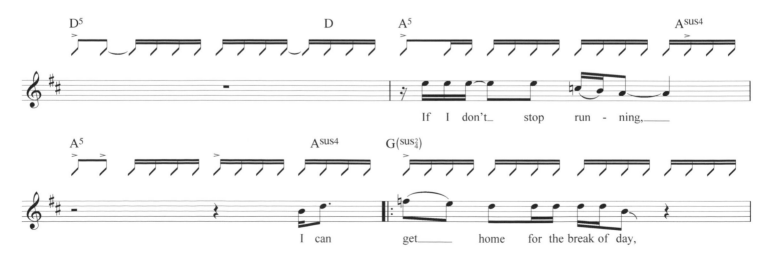

If I don't— stop run - ning,—

I can get— home for the break of day,

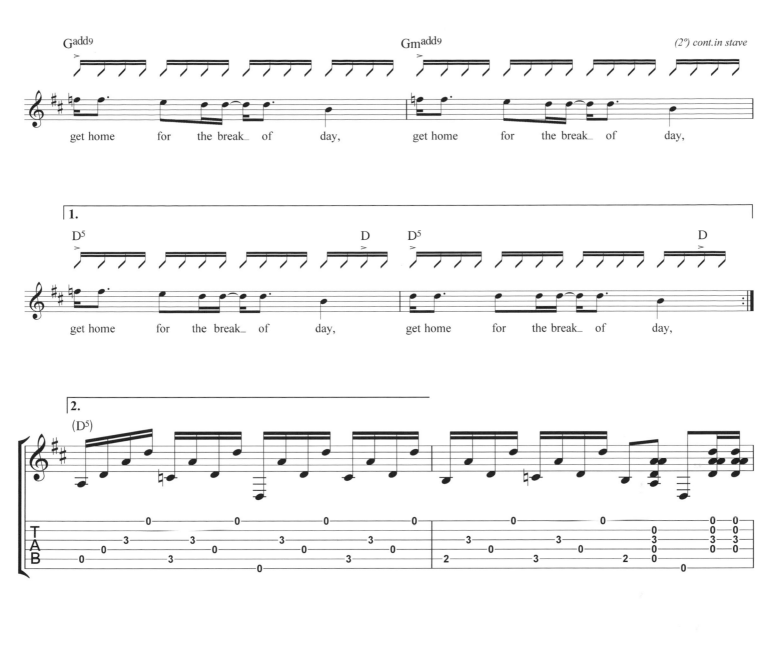

get home · · · for · the break _ of · day, · · · · · get home · · · for · the break _ of · day,

**1.**

get home · · · for · the break _ of · day, · · · · · get home · · · for · the break _ of · day,

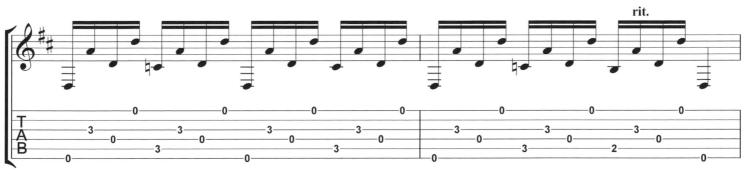

**2.**

# BANKER'S BLUES

Words & Music by Big Bill Broonzy

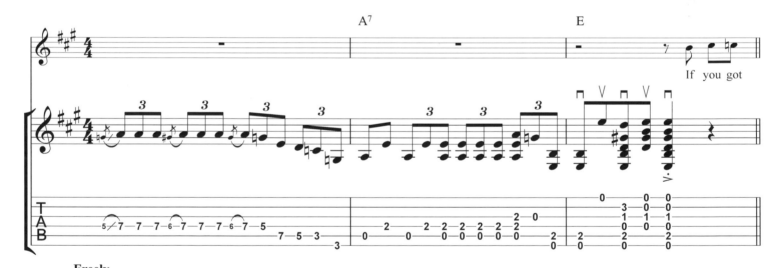

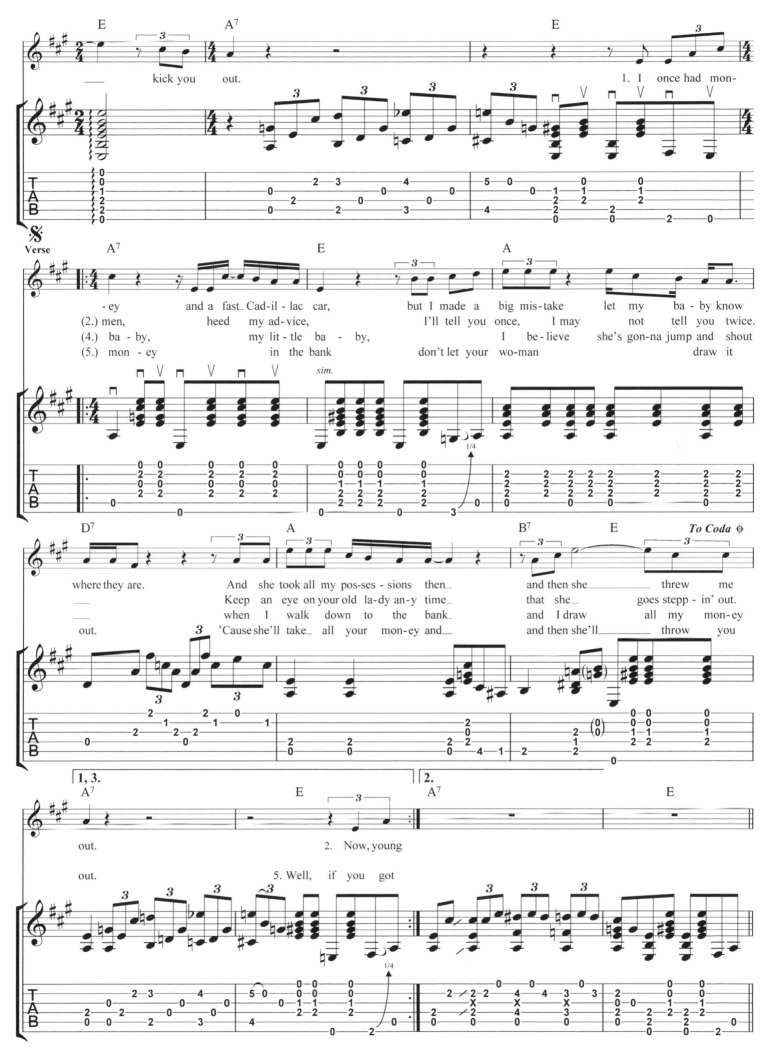

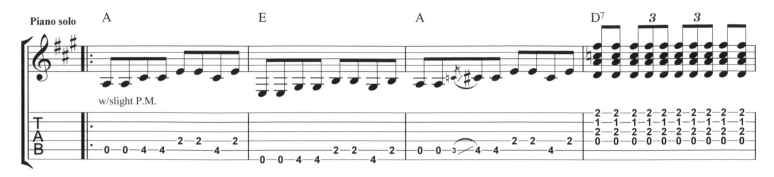

w/slight P.M.

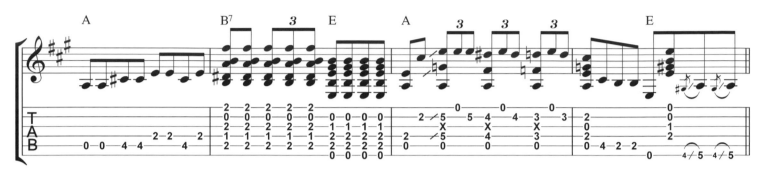

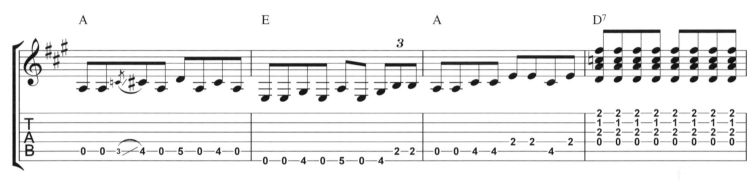

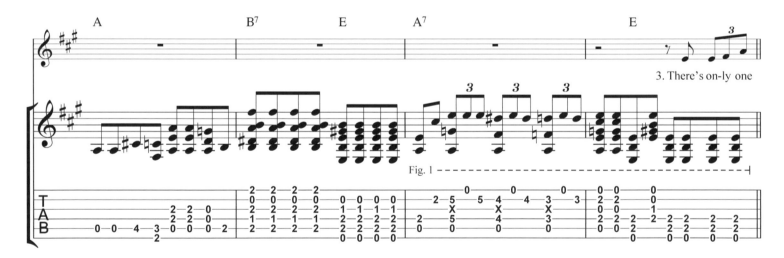

Fig. 1

3. There's on-ly one

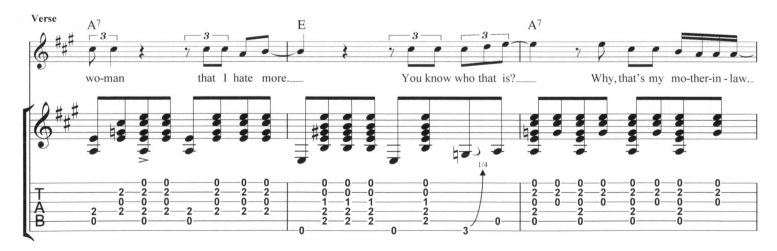

Verse

wo-man that I hate more.___ You know who that is?___ Why, that's my mo-ther-in-law.__

My ba-by's pret-ty fast, but her mo-ther's ev-en fast-er on the draw.

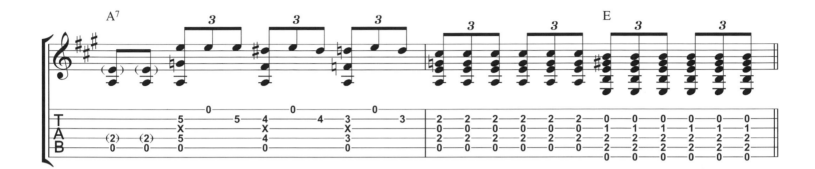

Solo

w/slide

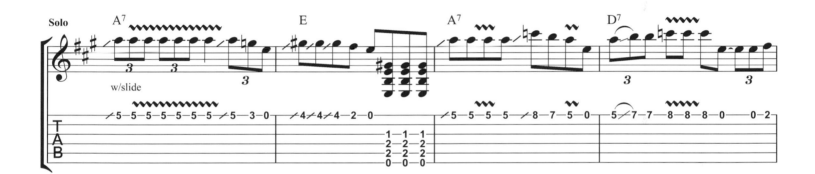

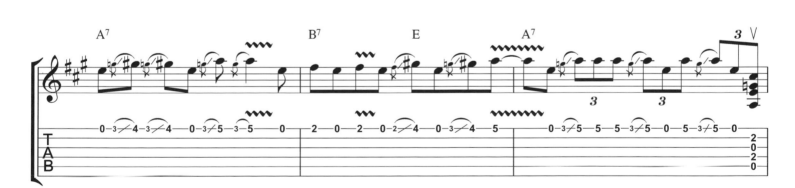

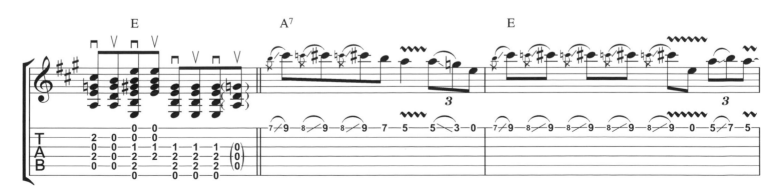

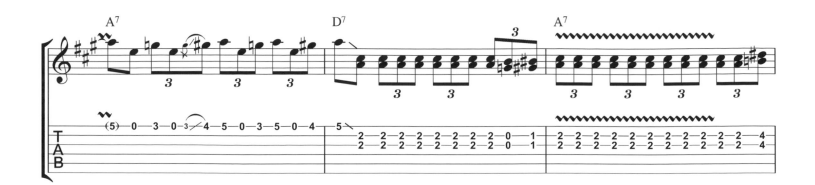

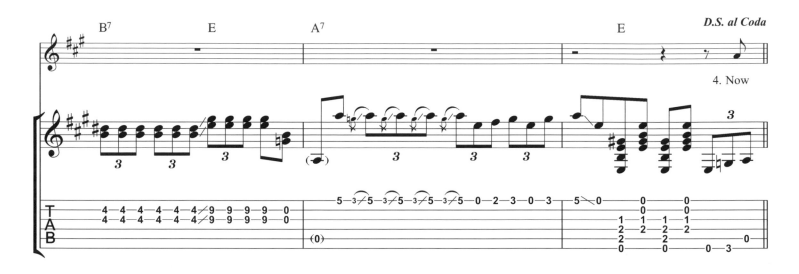

4. Now

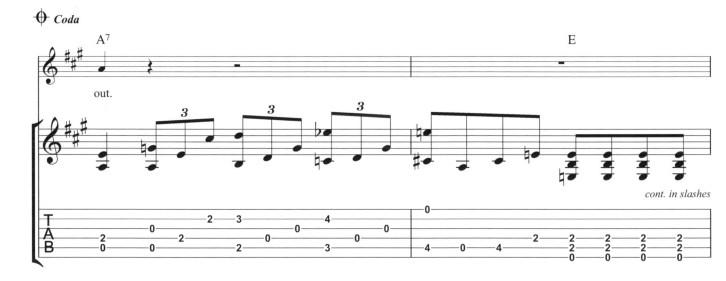

out.

cont. in slashes

**Harmonica solo**

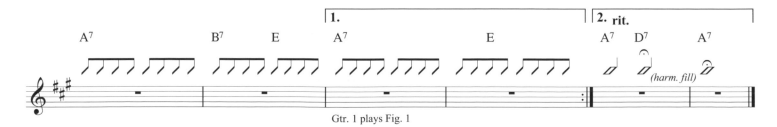

Gtr. 1 plays Fig. 1

# BRATCHA DUBHA

Music by Rory Gallagher

*chords imply overall harmony

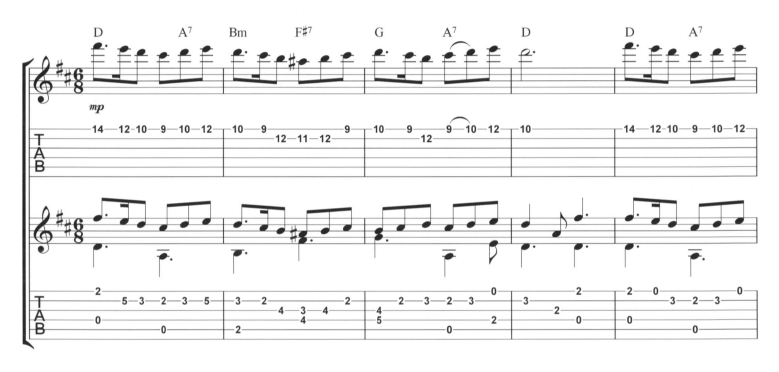

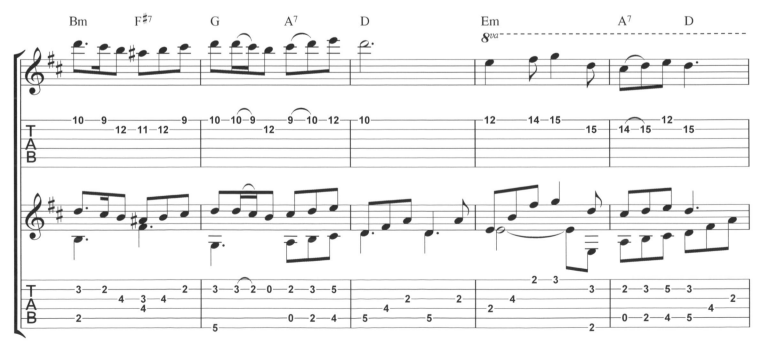

28

# THE CUCKOO

Words & Music by Rory Gallagher

ne - ver_____ hol - ler cuck - oo un - til the fourth_

Fig. 1 --------------------------------------------------------

(Em)

day (Am)

of Ju - ly. 2. Jack Of

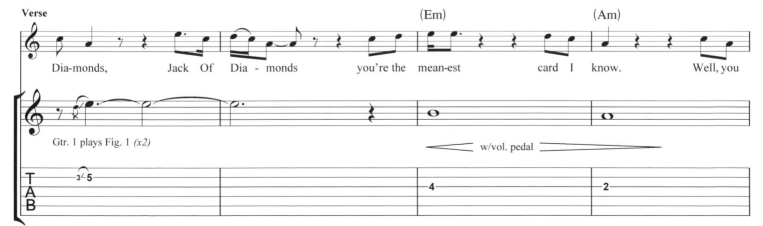

**Verse**

Dia-monds, Jack Of Dia - monds you're the mean-est (Em) card I know. (Am) Well, you

Gtr. 1 plays Fig. 1 *(x2)*

w/vol. pedal

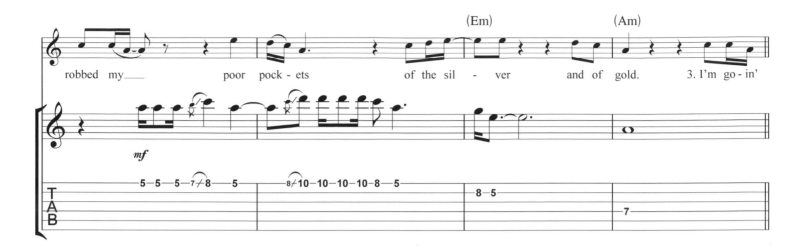

robbed my___ poor pock-ets of the sil - ver and of gold. 3. I'm go-in'

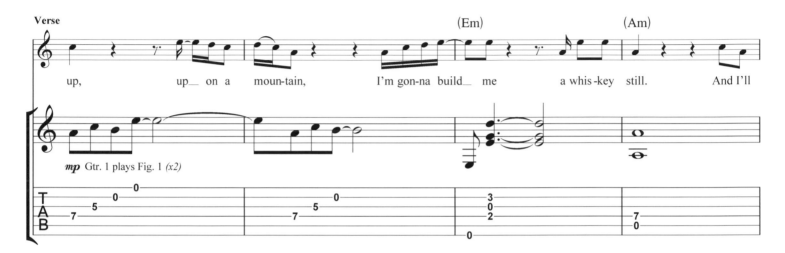

**Verse**

up, up___ on a moun-tain, I'm gon-na build___ me a whis-key still. And I'll

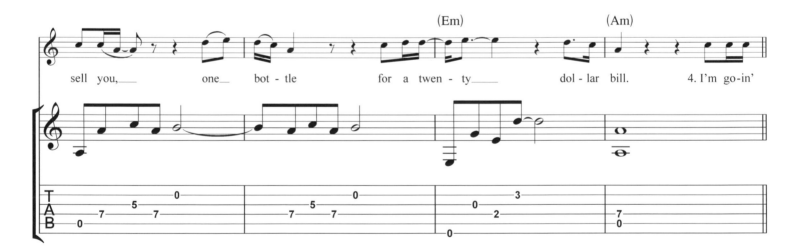

sell you,___ one___ bot - tle for a twen - ty___ dol - lar bill. 4. I'm go-in'

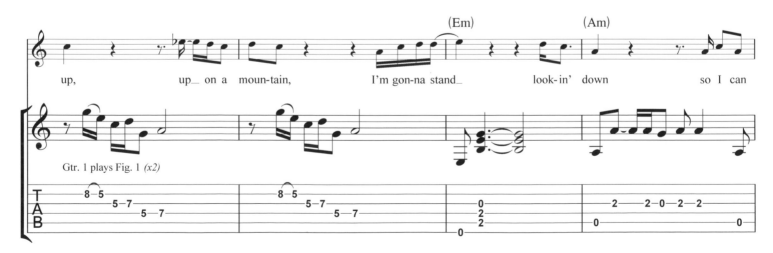

up, up___ on a moun-tain, I'm gon-na stand___ look-in' down so I can

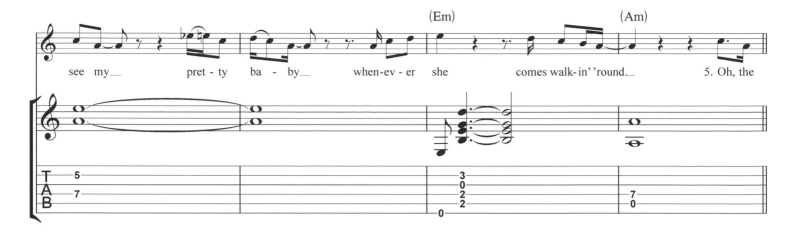

see my___ pret - ty ba - by___ when-ev - er she comes walk-in' 'round.___ 5. Oh, the

(Em)          (Am)

**Verse**

cuck-oo, she's a pret-ty bird, and she war-bles as she flies. But she

Gtr. 1 plays Fig. 1 *(x2)*

(Em)          (Am)

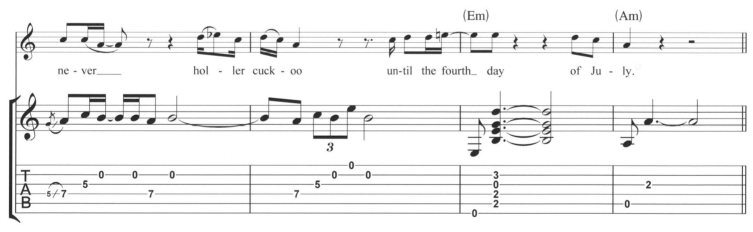

ne - ver___ hol - ler cuck - oo un-til the fourth_ day of Ju - ly.

(Em)          (Am)

**Solo**
**Gtr. 1** (C)          (G)          (Am)          (C)          (G)          (Am)

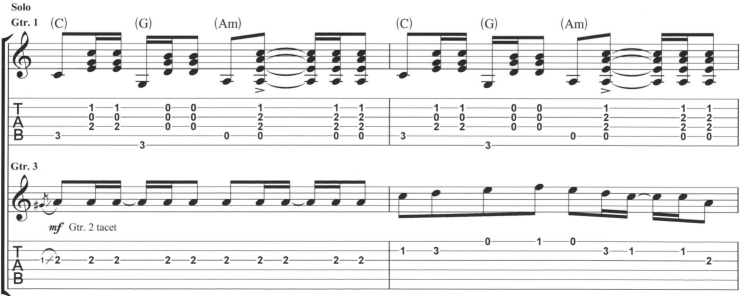

**Gtr. 3**

*mf* Gtr. 2 tacet

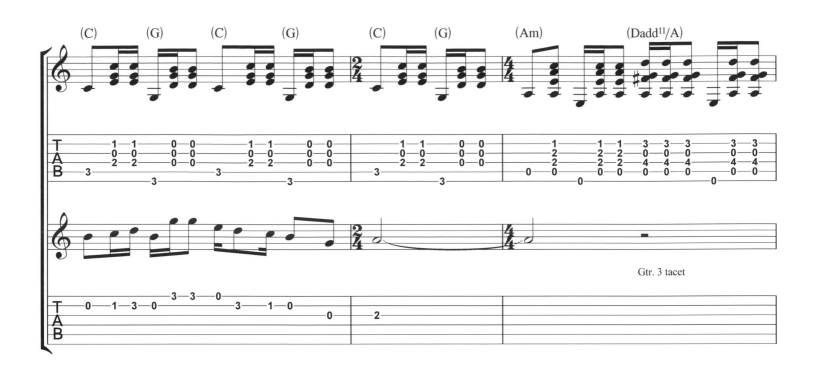

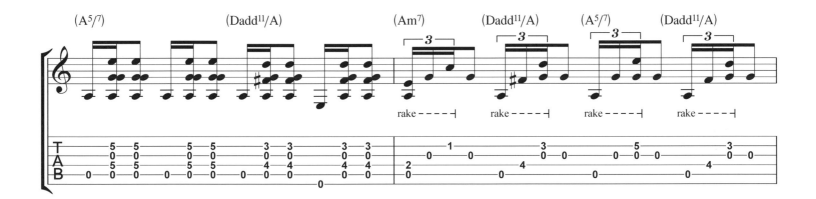

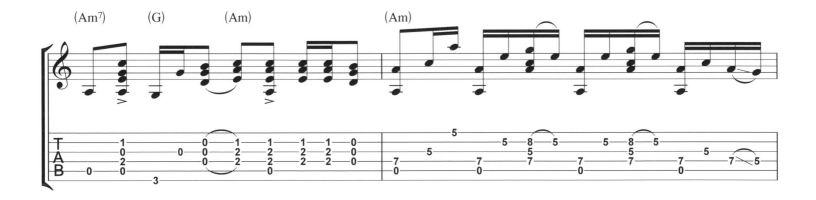

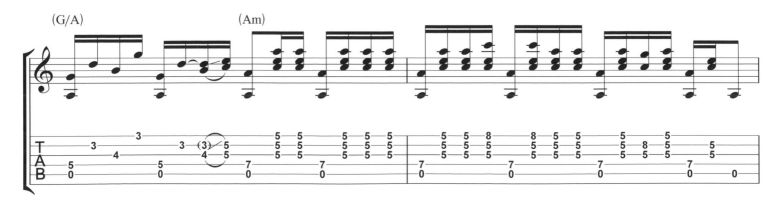

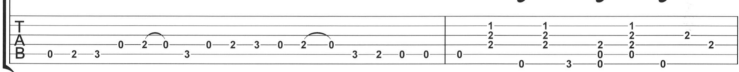

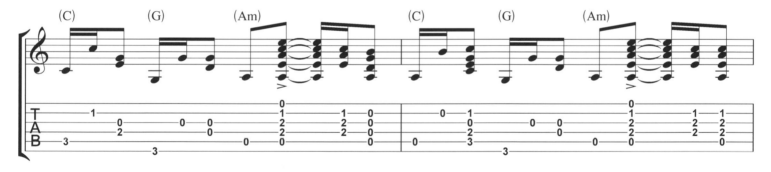

6. Well, I'll eat_

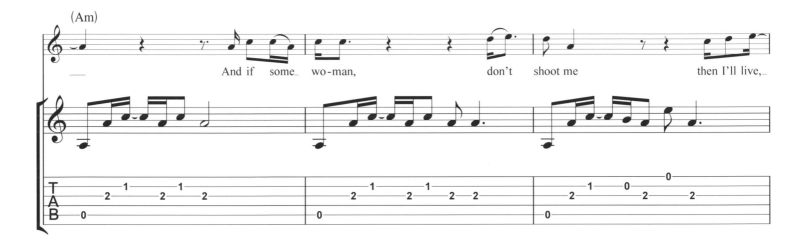

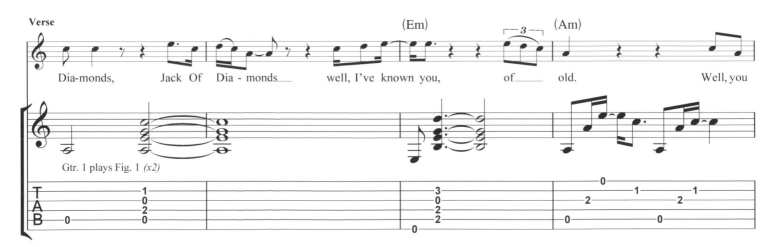

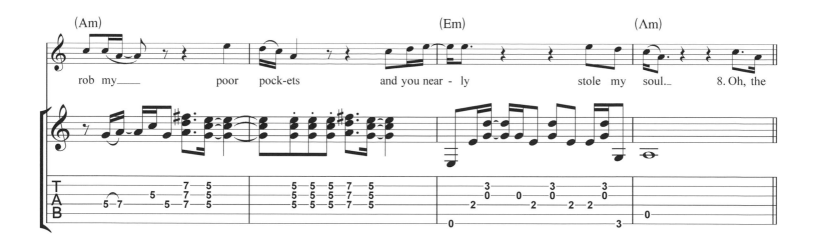

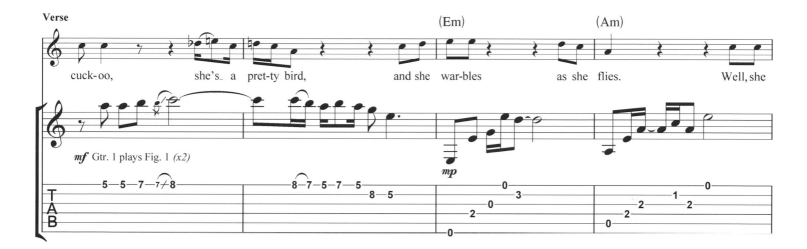

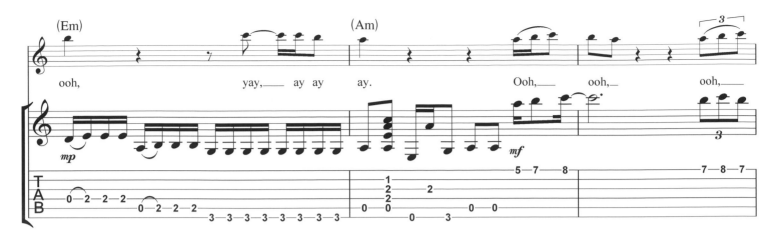

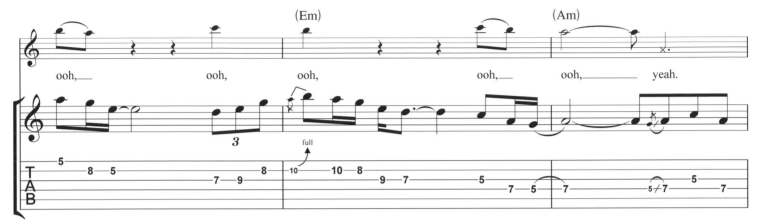

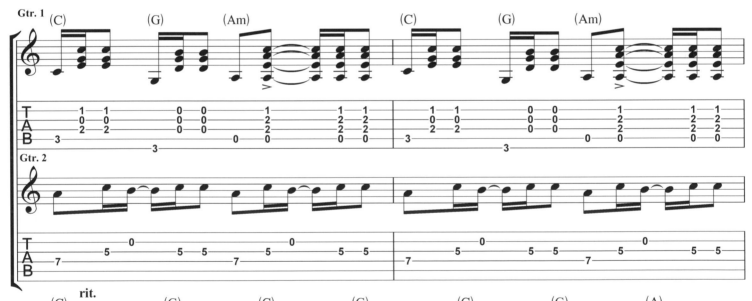

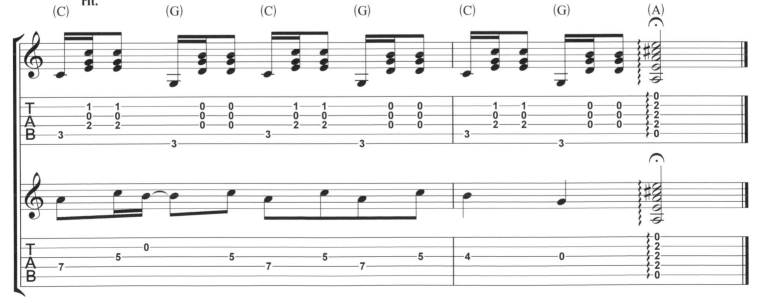

# EMPIRE STATE EXPRESS

Words & Music by Eddie J. House Jnr.

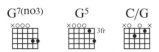

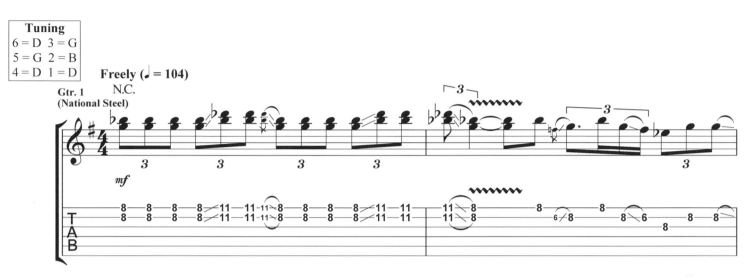

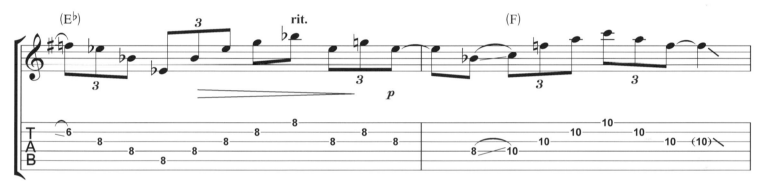

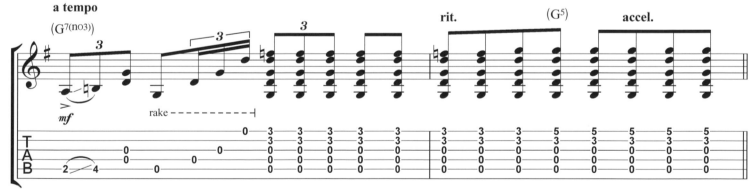

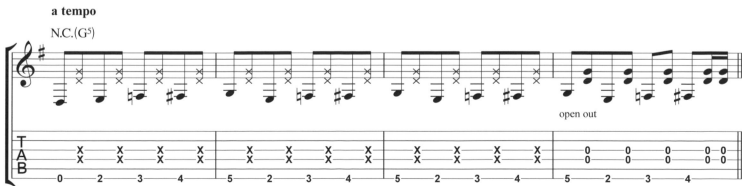

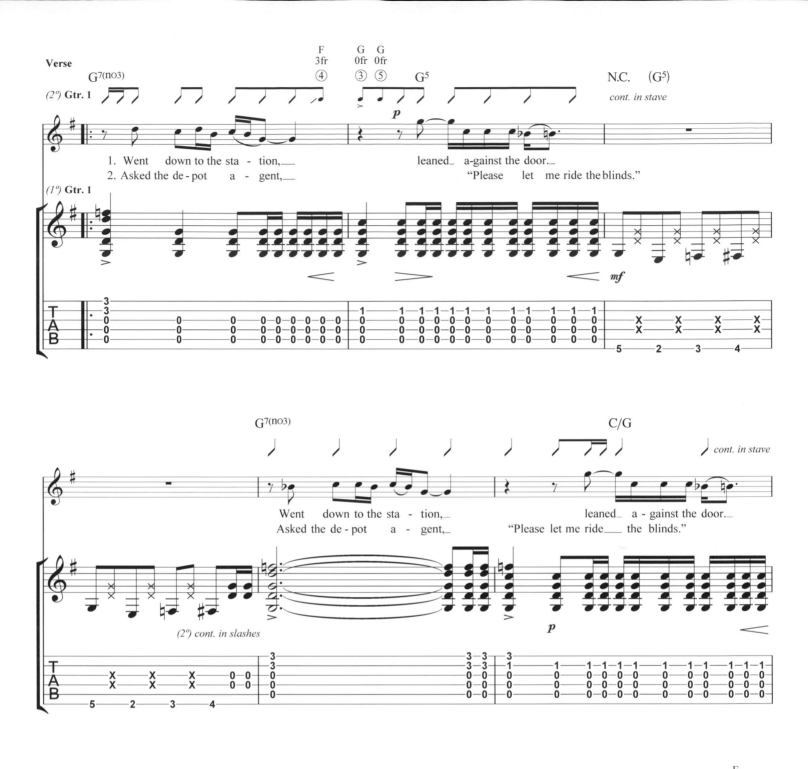

1. Went down to the sta - tion,___  leaned___ a-gainst the door.___
2. Asked the de - pot a - gent,___  "Please let me ride the blinds."

Went down to the sta - tion,___  leaned___ a - gainst the door.___
Asked the de - pot a - gent,___  "Please let me ride___ the blinds."

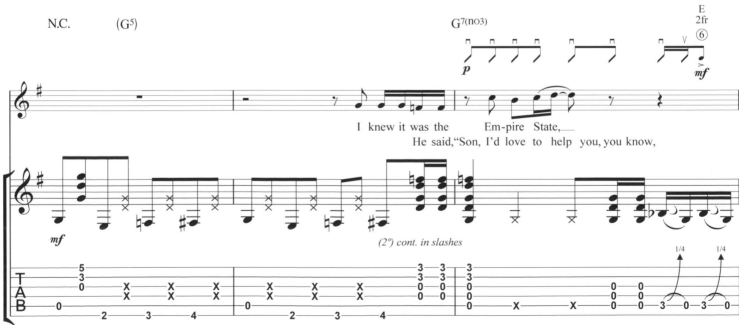

I knew it was the Em-pire State,___
He said, "Son, I'd love to help you, you know,

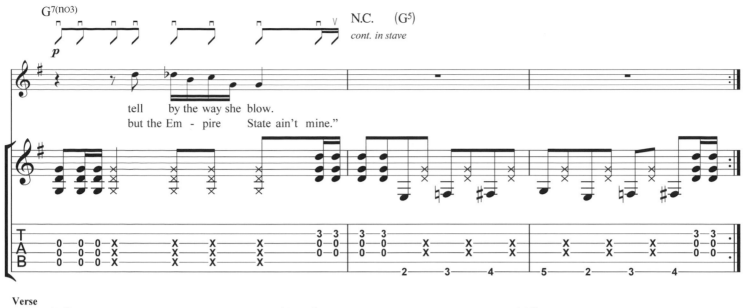

tell    by the way she blow.
but the Em - pire    State ain't mine."

**Verse**

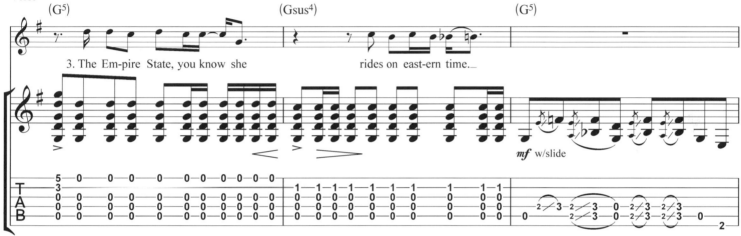

3. The Em-pire State, you know she    rides on east-ern time.__

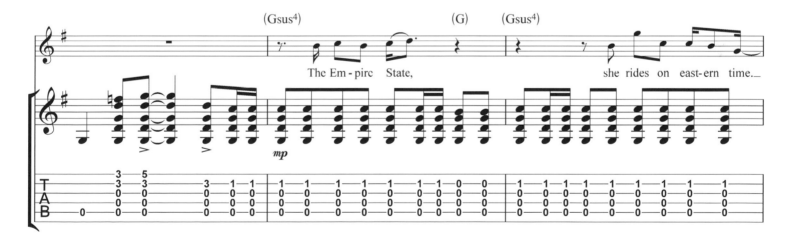

The Em - pire    State,    she rides on east-ern time.__

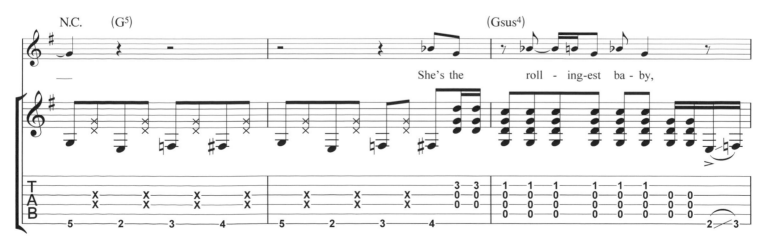

She's the    roll - ing-est ba - by,

41

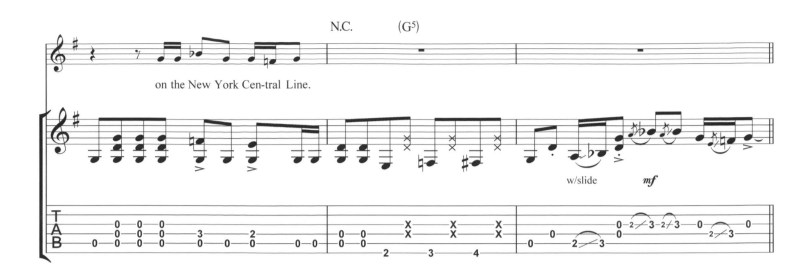

on the New York Cen-tral Line.

**Solo**

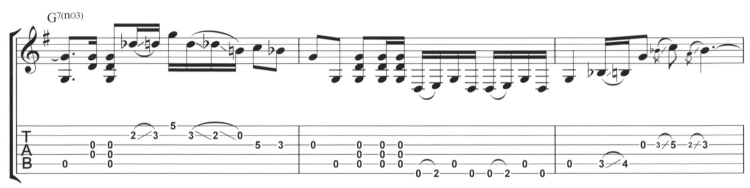

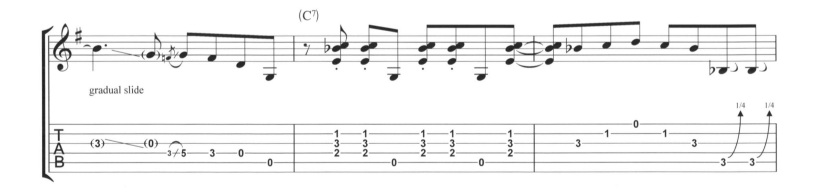

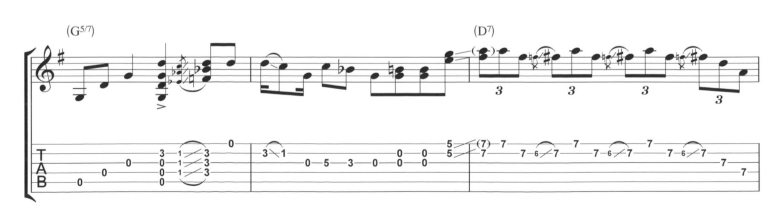

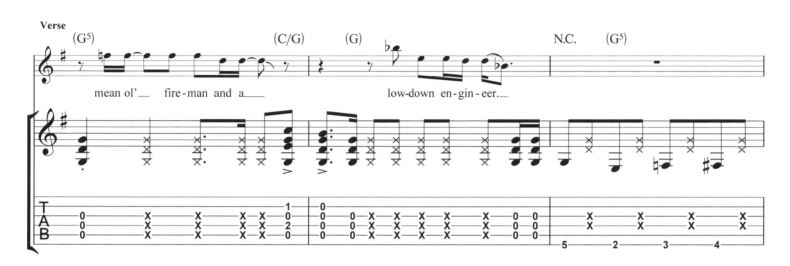

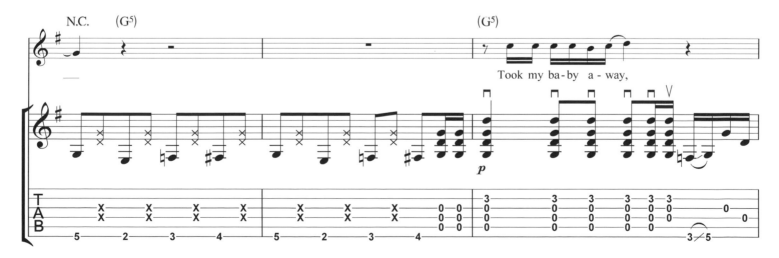

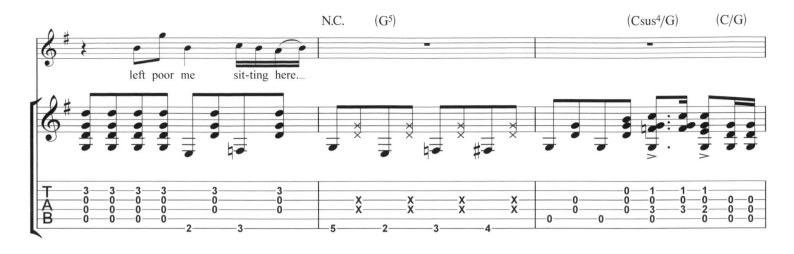

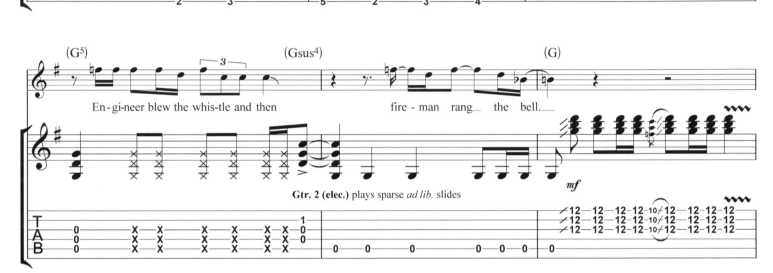

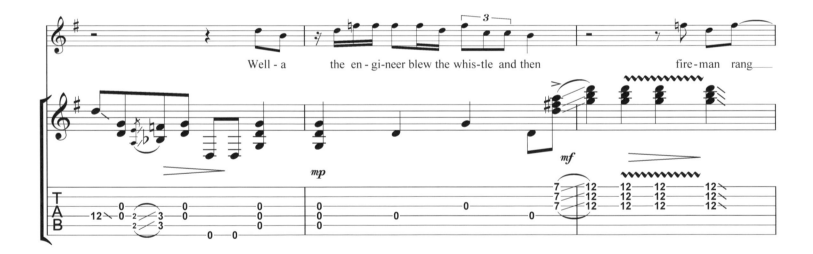

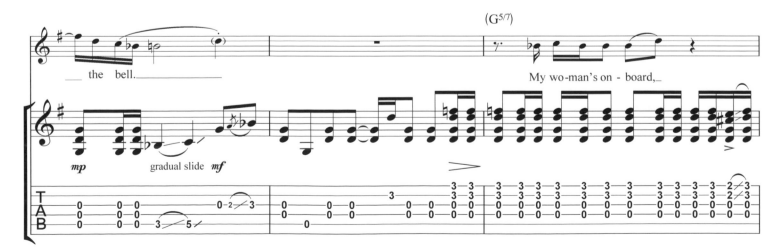

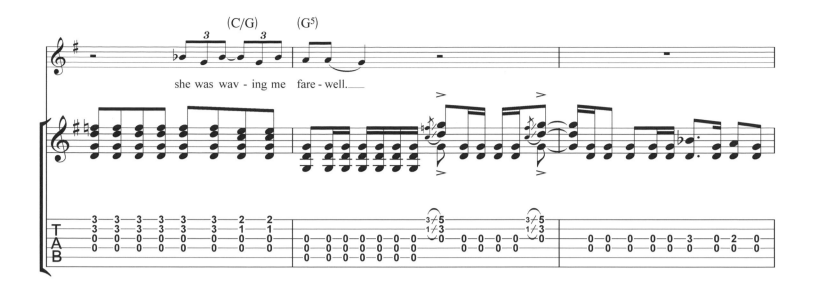

she was wav - ing me fare - well.____

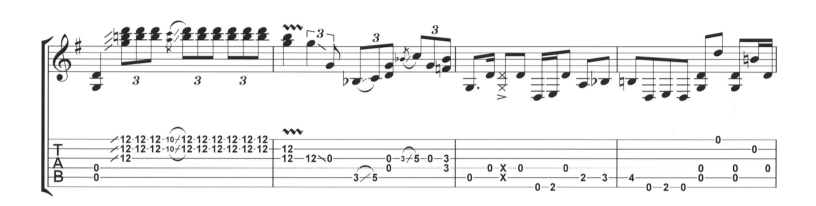

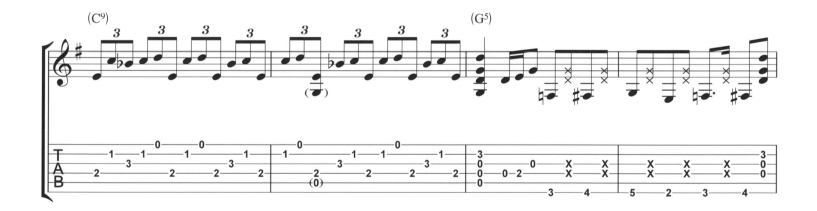

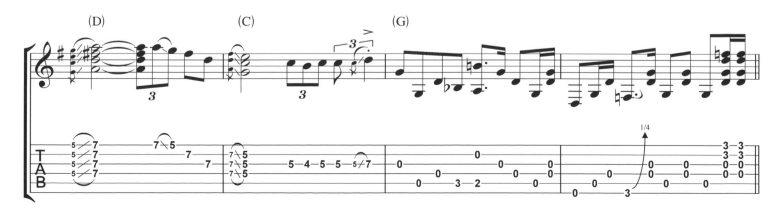

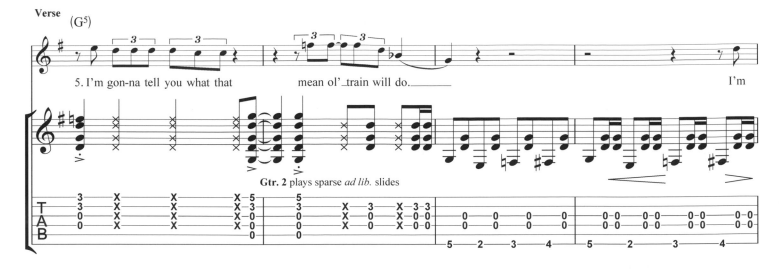

**Verse** (G5)

5. I'm gon-na tell you what that mean ol' train will do._____ I'm

**Gtr. 2** plays sparse *ad lib.* slides

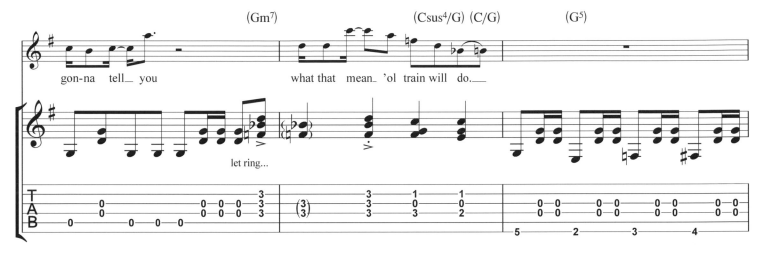

(Gm7)  (Csus4/G) (C/G)  (G5)

gon-na tell_ you what that mean_ 'ol train will do.____

let ring...

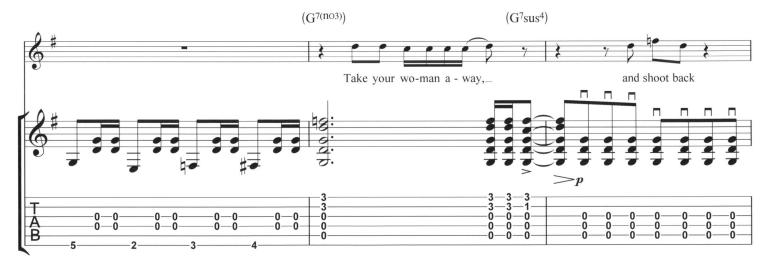

(G7(no3))  (G7sus4)

Take your wo-man a - way,____  and shoot back

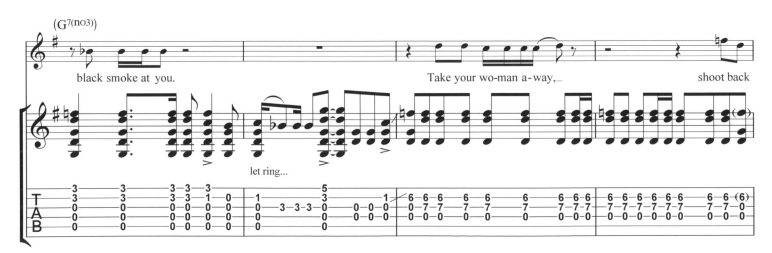

(G7(no3))

black smoke at you.  Take your wo-man a-way,____  shoot back

let ring...

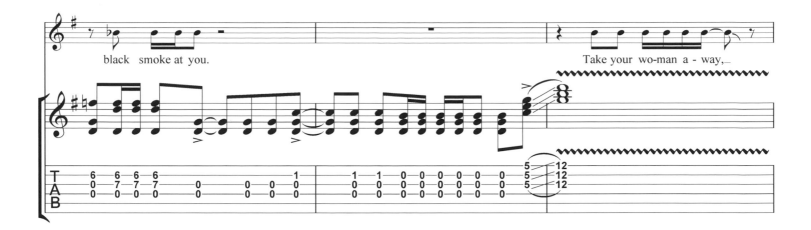

black smoke at you.

Take your wo-man a - way,___

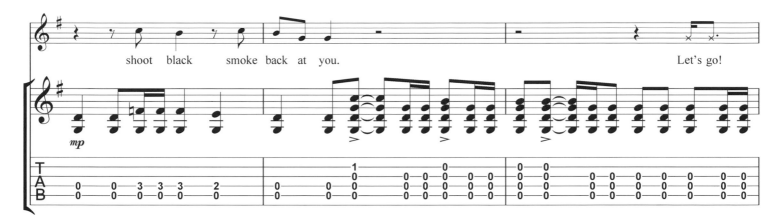

shoot black    smoke back at    you.

Let's go!

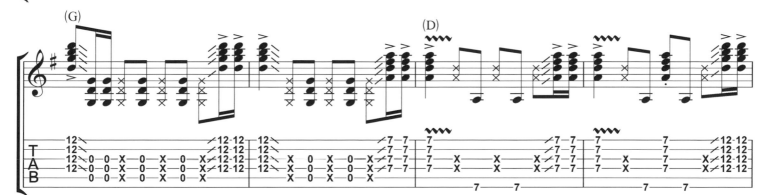

(G)

(D)

(G)

(D)    (C)    (G5)

rall.

gradual slide

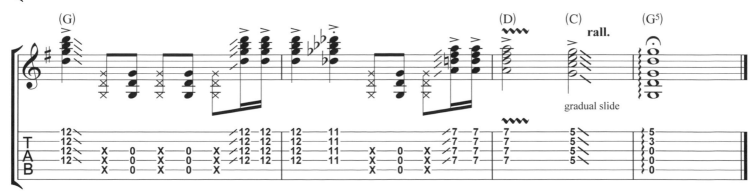

# DON'T KNOW WHERE I'M GOING

Words & Music by Rory Gallagher

To match original recording tune guitar down a semitone

**Intro**

♩ = 102

Gtr. 1 (12 str. steel str. acous.)

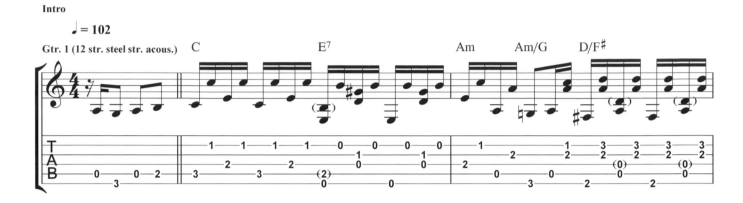

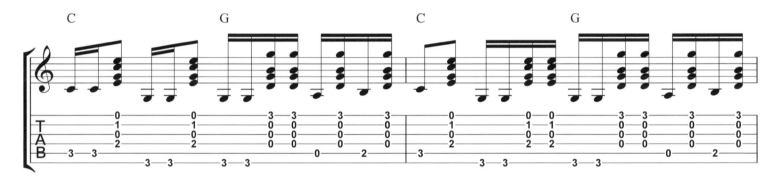

**Harmonica solo**

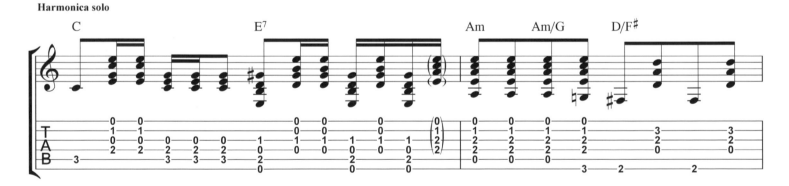

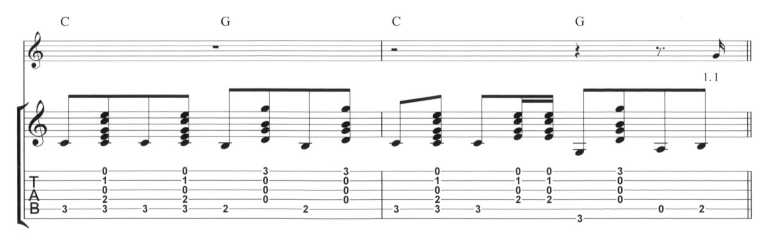

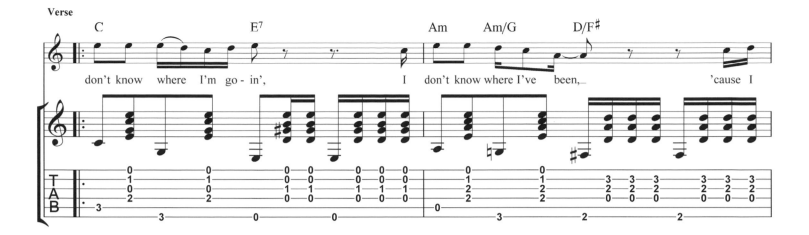

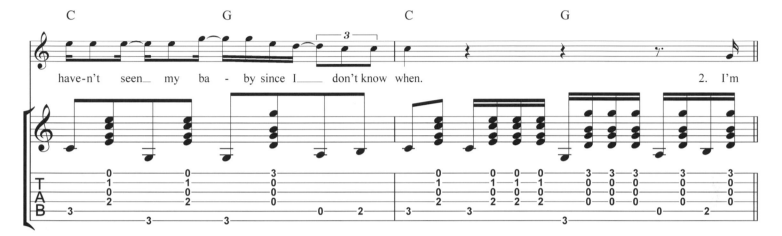

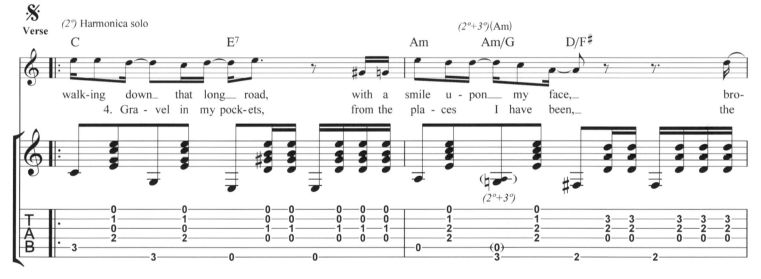

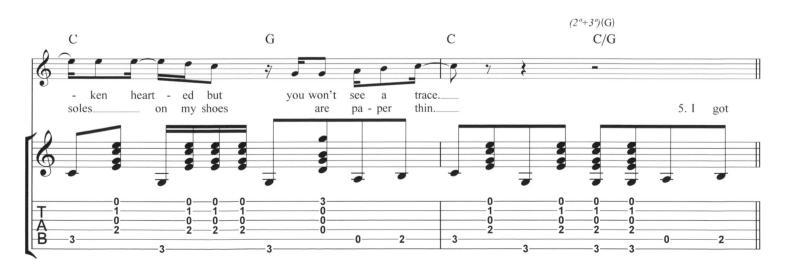

49

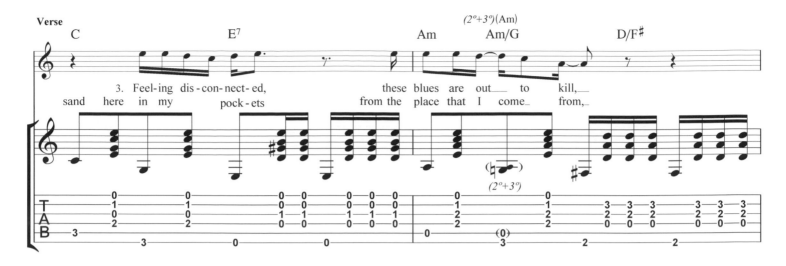

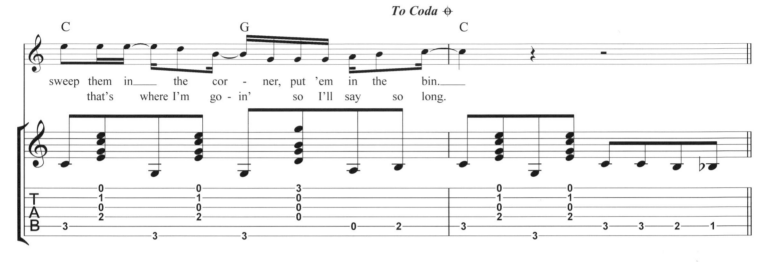

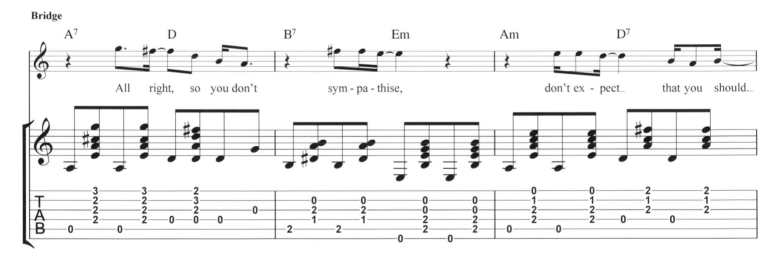

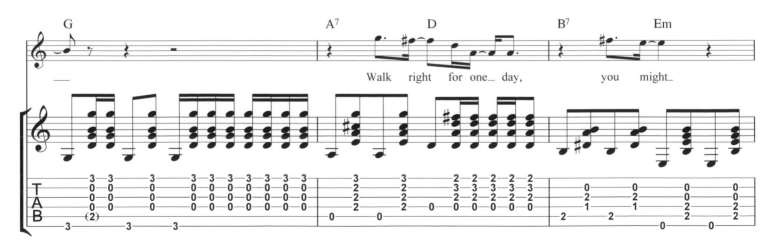

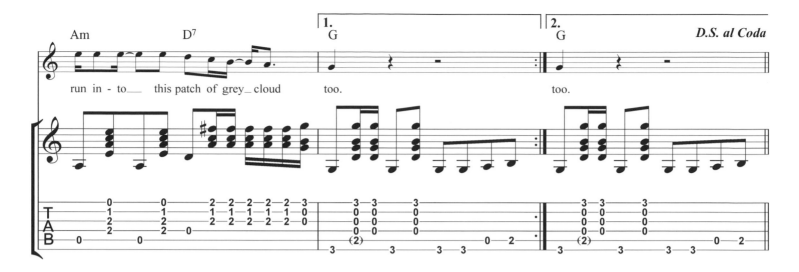

run in - to___ this patch of grey___ cloud   too.                    too.

Coda

Harmonica solo

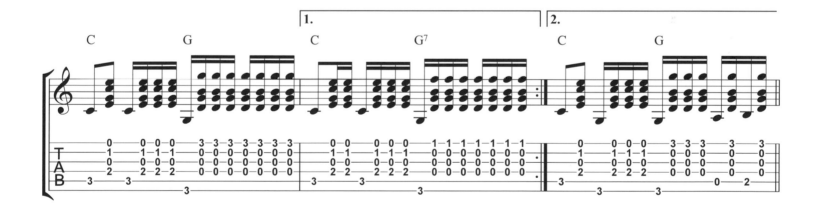

Repeat ad lib. to fade

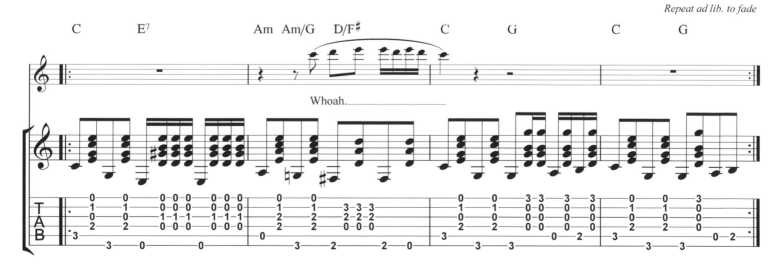

Whoah._____

# GOING TO MY HOME TOWN (LIVE)

Words & Music by Rory Gallagher

made a mis-take, I moved much too far, and now I know__ what the lone-some blues are.

(G) (D)

I'm get-tin' lone-some, I'm get-tin' blue, I need some-one__ to talk to.__

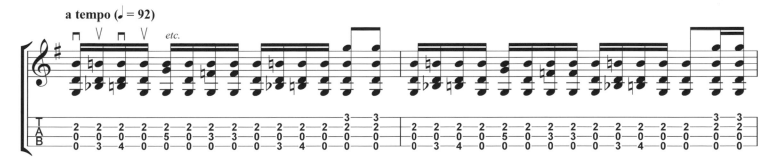

(G)

I'm get-tin' lone-some, I'm get-tin' blue, Let me tell you where I'm go-in' to. Yeah.

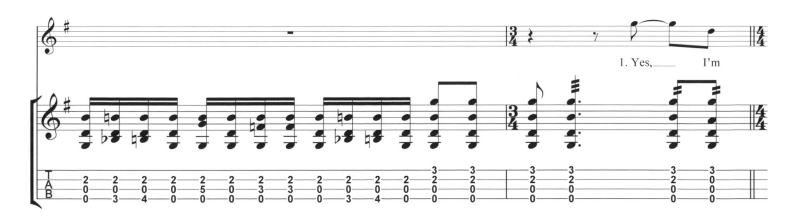

a tempo (♩ = 92)

1. Yes,__ I'm

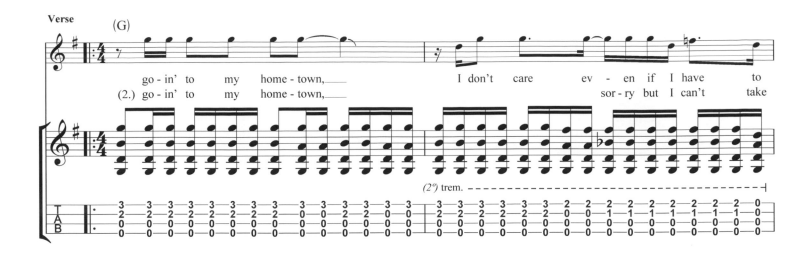

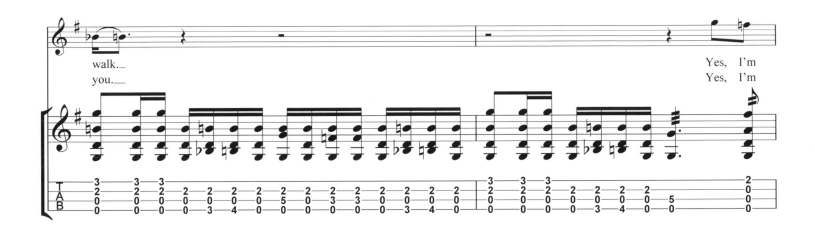

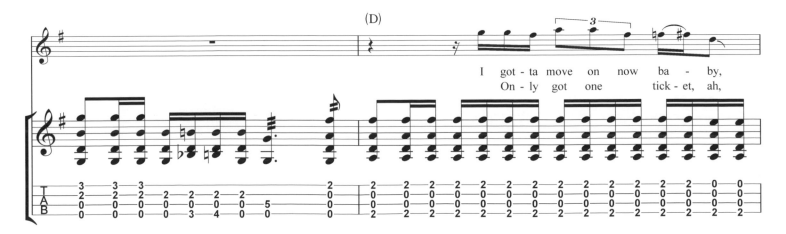

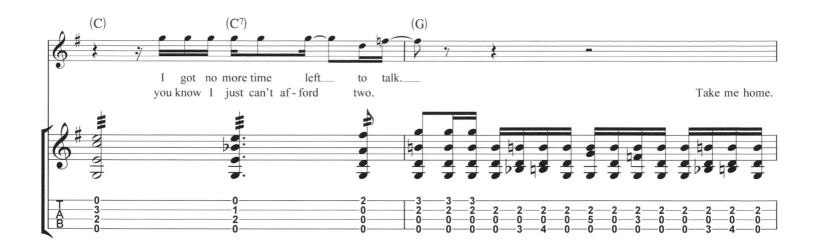

I got no more time left to talk.
you know I just can't af-ford two.

Take me home.

2. Yes, I'm

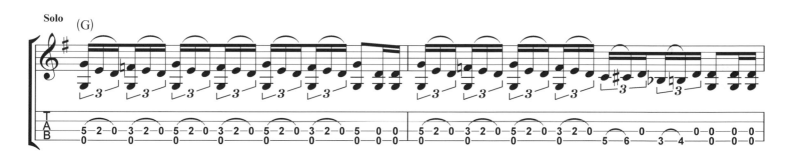

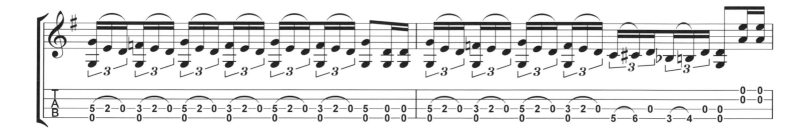

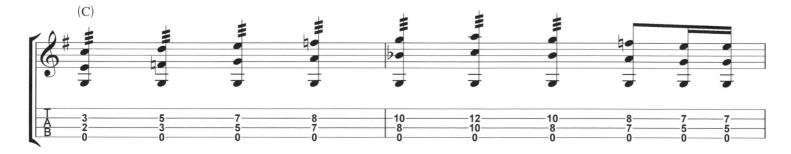

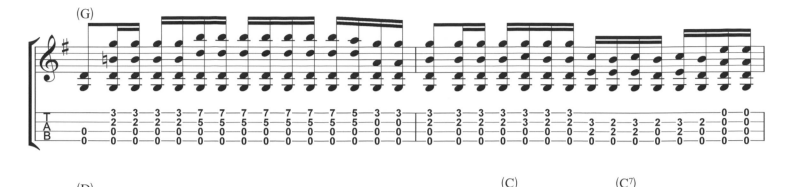

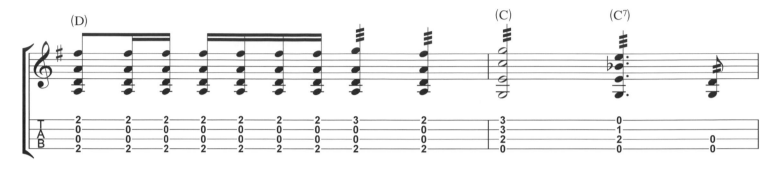

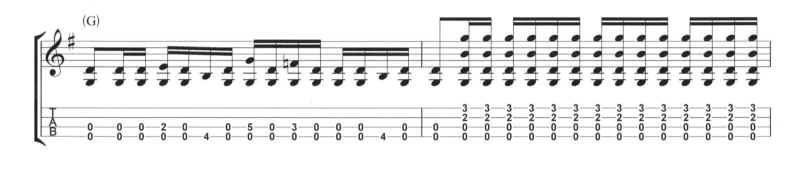

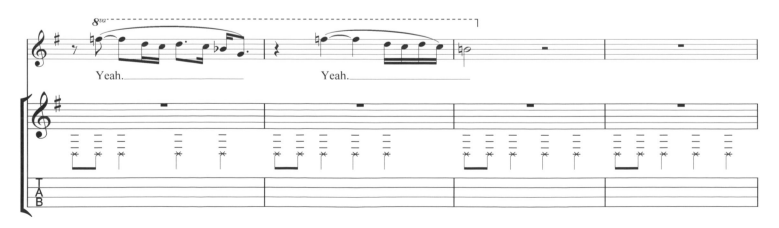

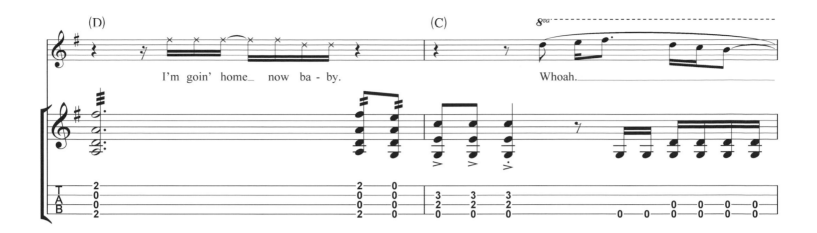

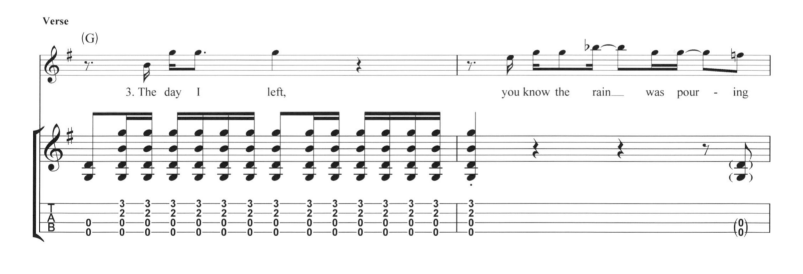

**Verse**

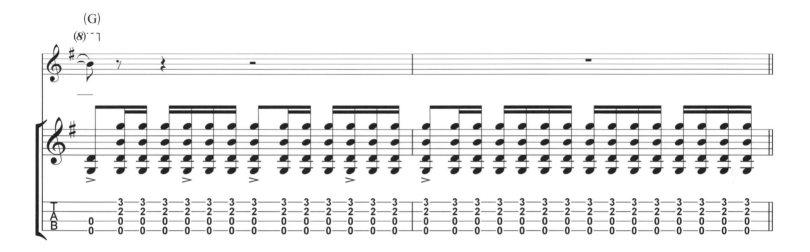

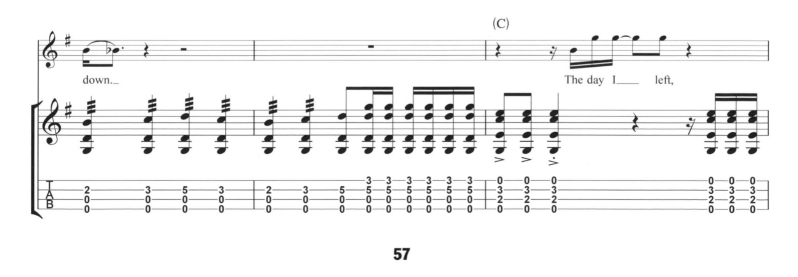

57

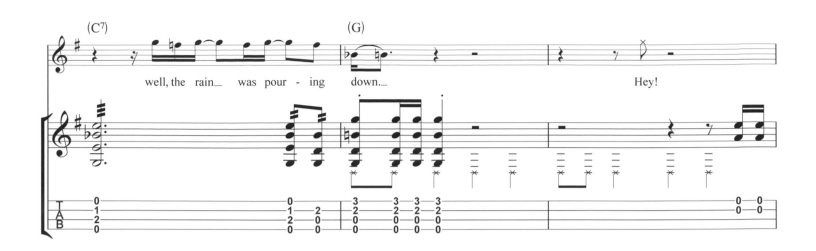

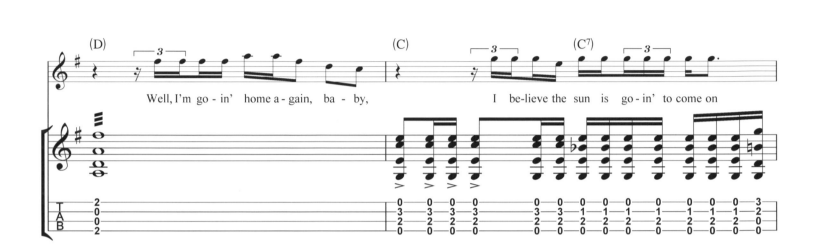

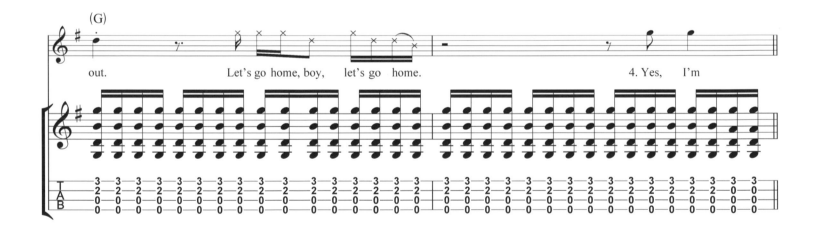

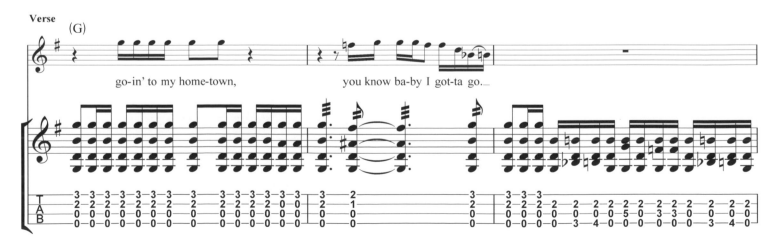

58

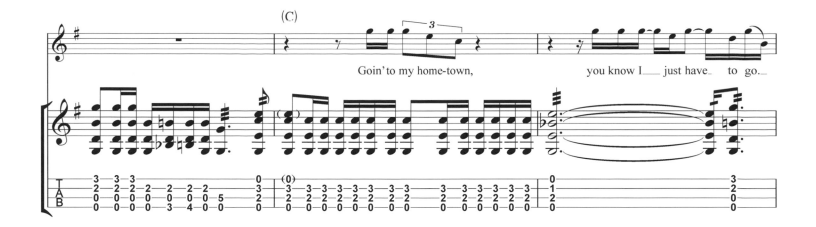

Goin' to my home-town, you know I ___ just have ___ to go. ___

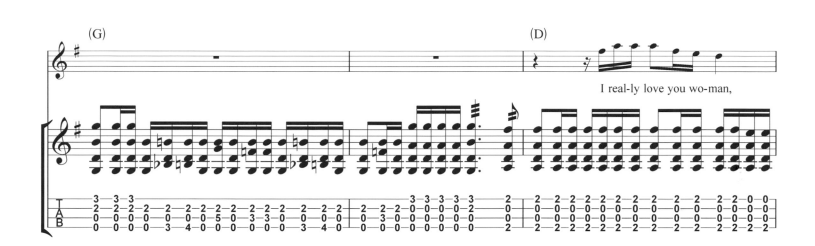

I real-ly love you wo-man,

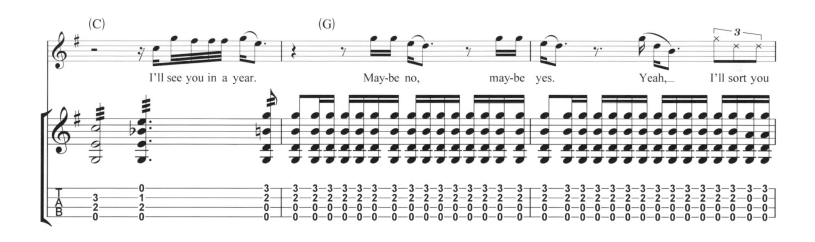

I'll see you in a year. May-be no, may-be yes. Yeah, ___ I'll sort you

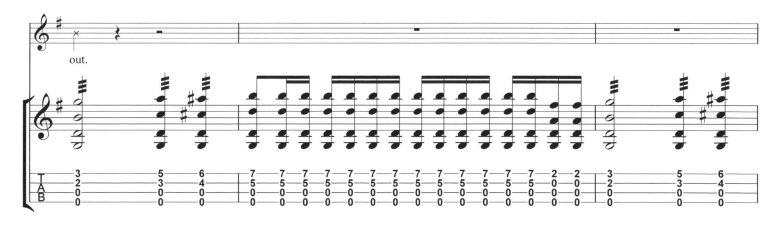

out.

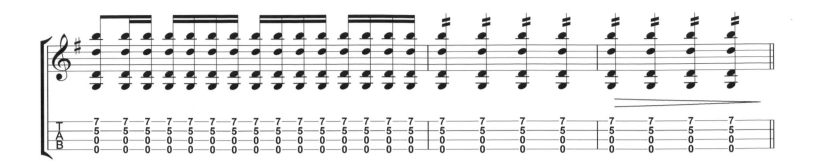

**Outro**

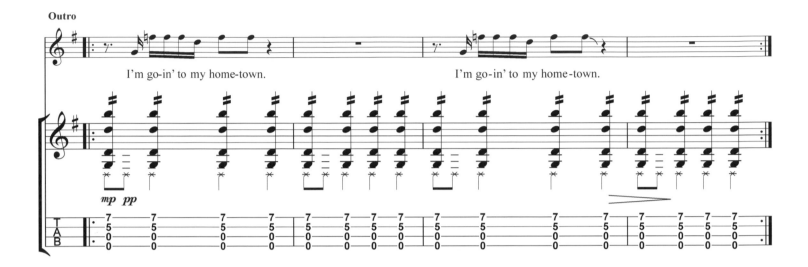

I'm go-in' to my home-town.

I'm go-in' to my home-town.

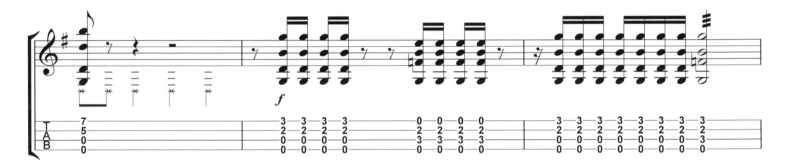

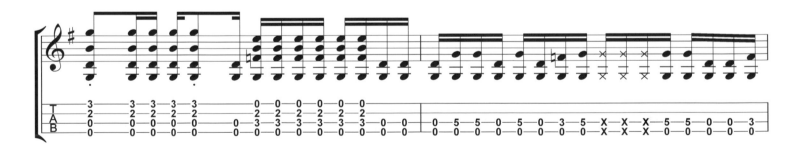

Yeah, ah

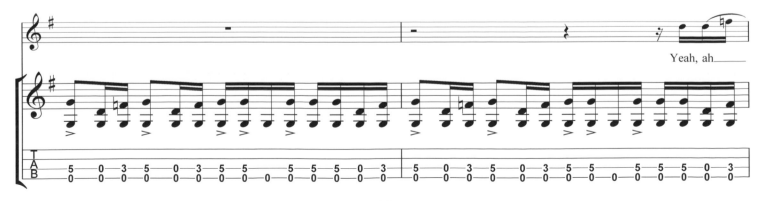

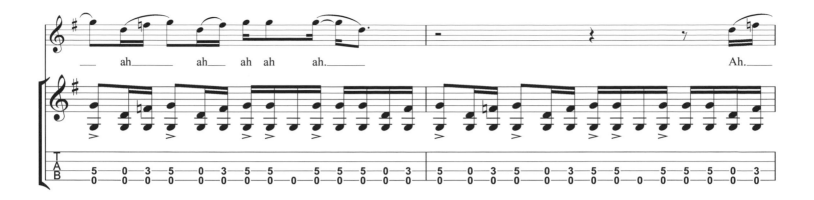

ah_____ ah___ ah ah ah._____ Ah._____

_____ Hey, hey hey. Hey, hey hey, hey, hey, hey,_____ hey.

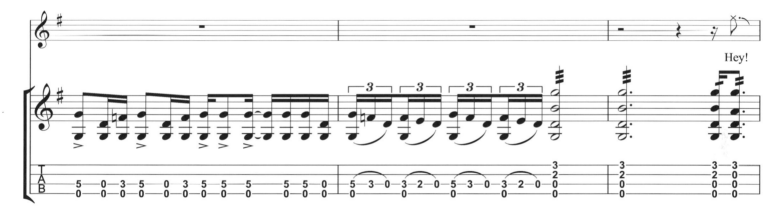

Hey!

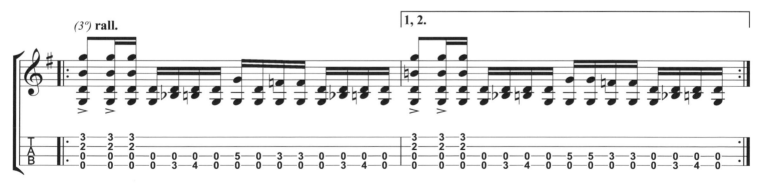

*(3ª)* **rall.** **1, 2.**

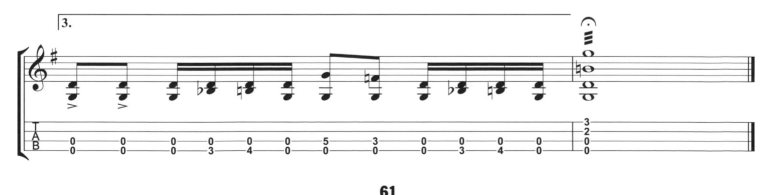

**3.**

# I'LL ADMIT YOU'RE GONE

Words & Music by Rory Gallagher

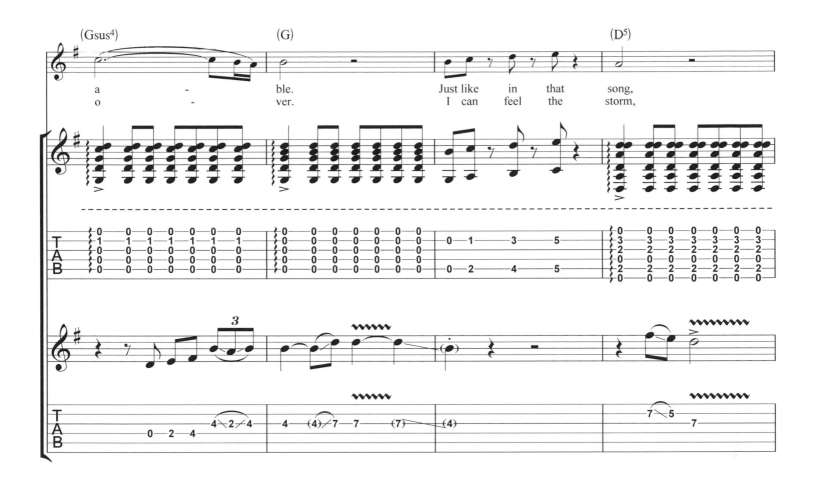

a - ble.  Just like in that song,
o - ver.  I can feel the storm,

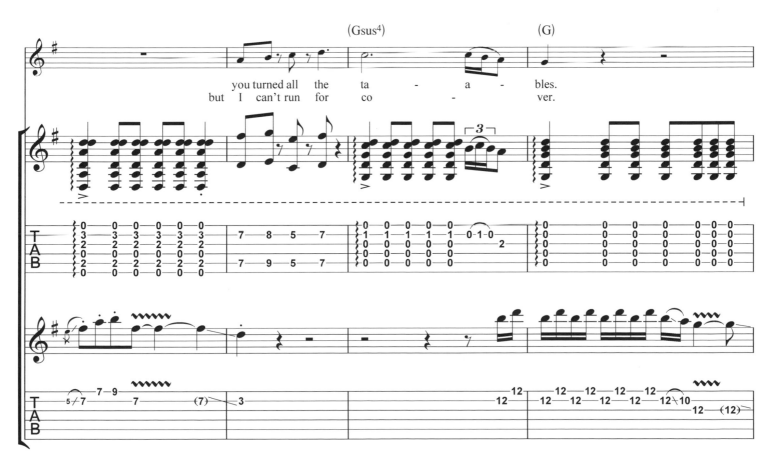

you turned all the ta - a - bles.
but I can't run for co - ver.

Now I know I'm wrong,
Where do I be - long,
life is hard to
I just keep on

shoul - der.
search - ing.
I won't last too long,
I want to see the dawn

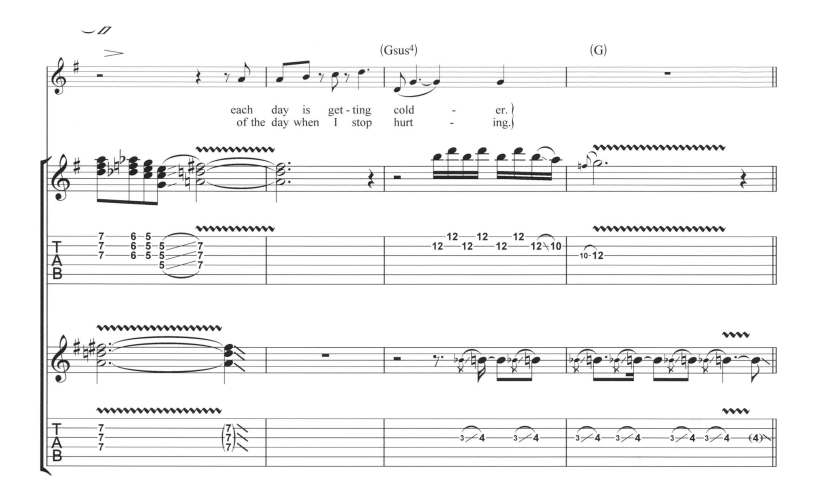

(Gsus⁴)

(G)

each day is get-ting cold - er.
of the day when I stop hurt - ing.

**Chorus**

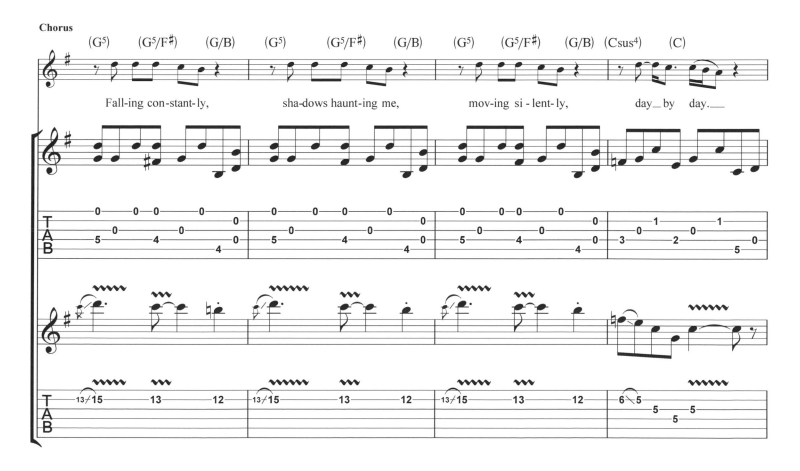

(G⁵)  (G⁵/F♯)  (G/B)  (G⁵)  (G⁵/F♯)  (G/B)  (G⁵)  (G⁵/F♯)  (G/B)  (Csus⁴)  (C)

Fall-ing con-stant-ly,  sha-dows haunt-ing me,  mov-ing si - lent-ly,  day__ by day.__

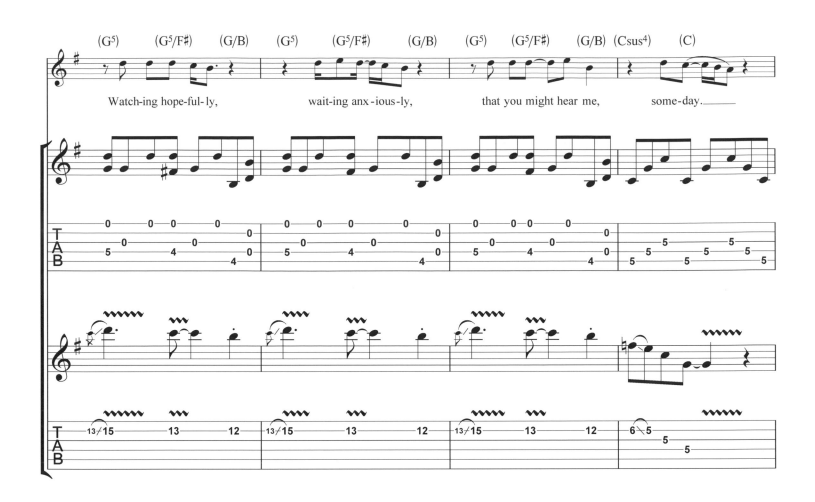

Watch-ing hope-ful-ly, wait-ing anx-ious-ly, that you might hear me, some-day.___

*To Coda*

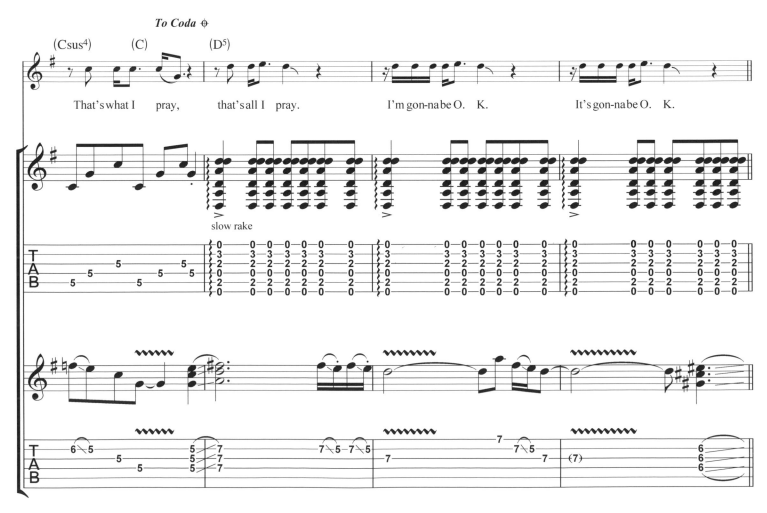

That's what I pray, that's all I pray. I'm gon-na be O. K. It's gon-na be O. K.

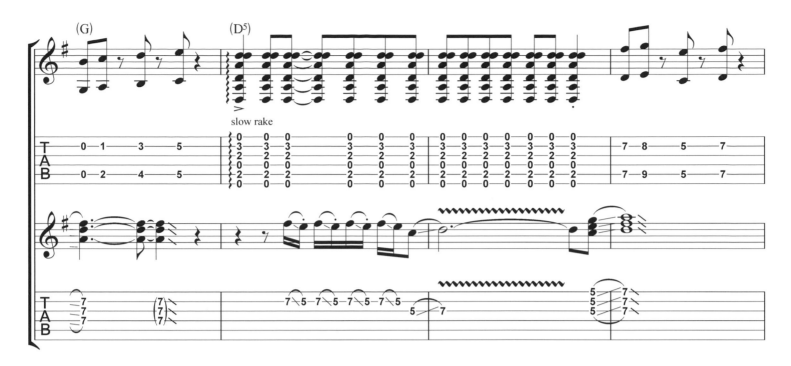

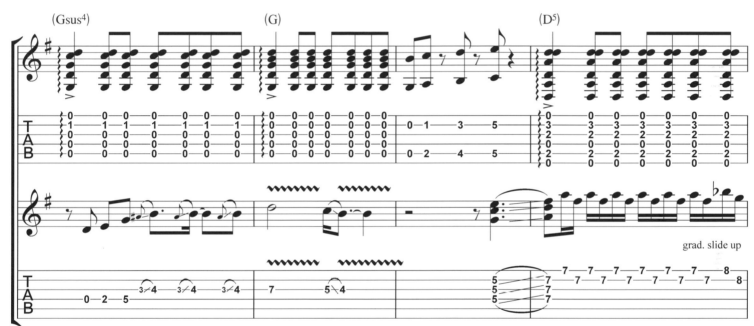

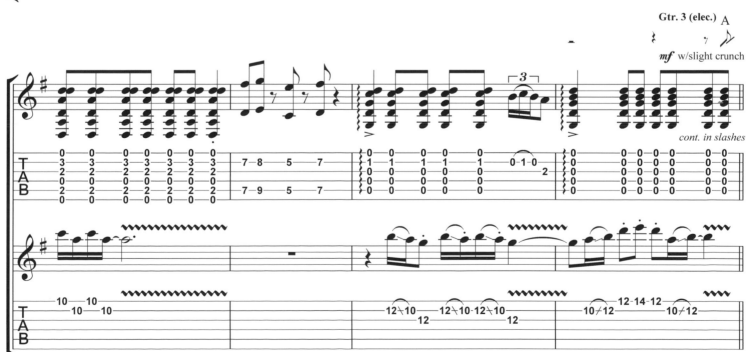

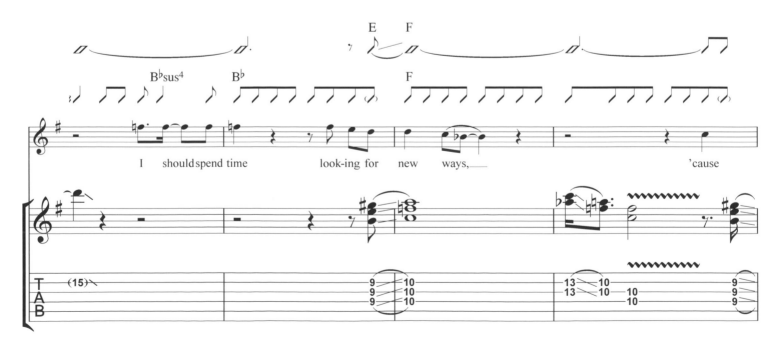

68

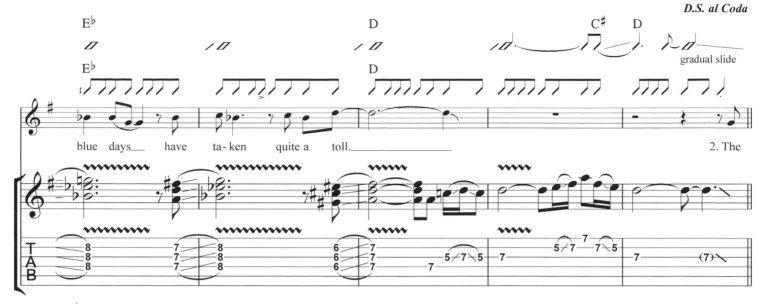

blue days___ have ta-ken quite a toll._____ 2. The

**Coda**

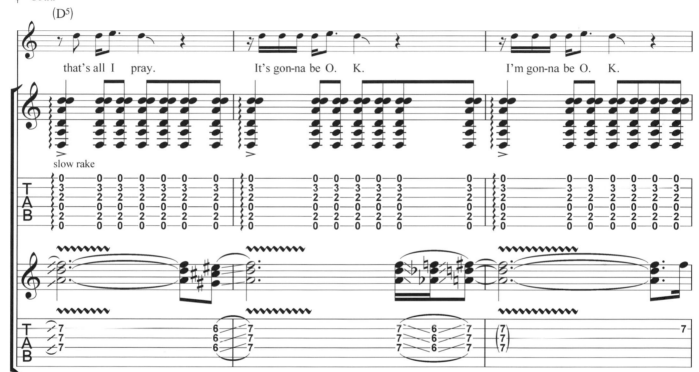

that's all I pray. It's gon-na be O. K. I'm gon-na be O. K.

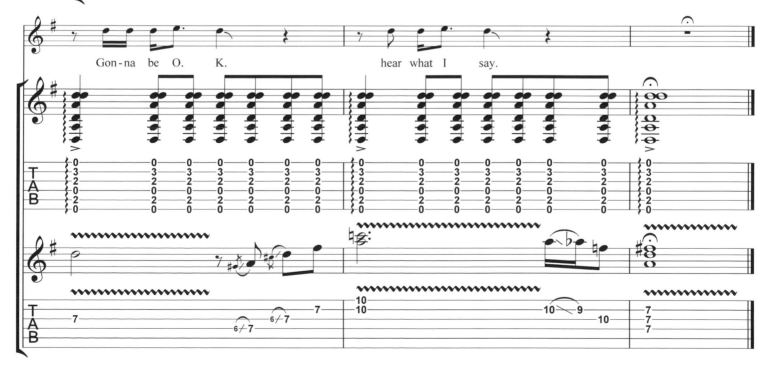

Gon-na be O. K. hear what I say.

# I'M NOT AWAKE YET

Words & Music by Rory Gallagher

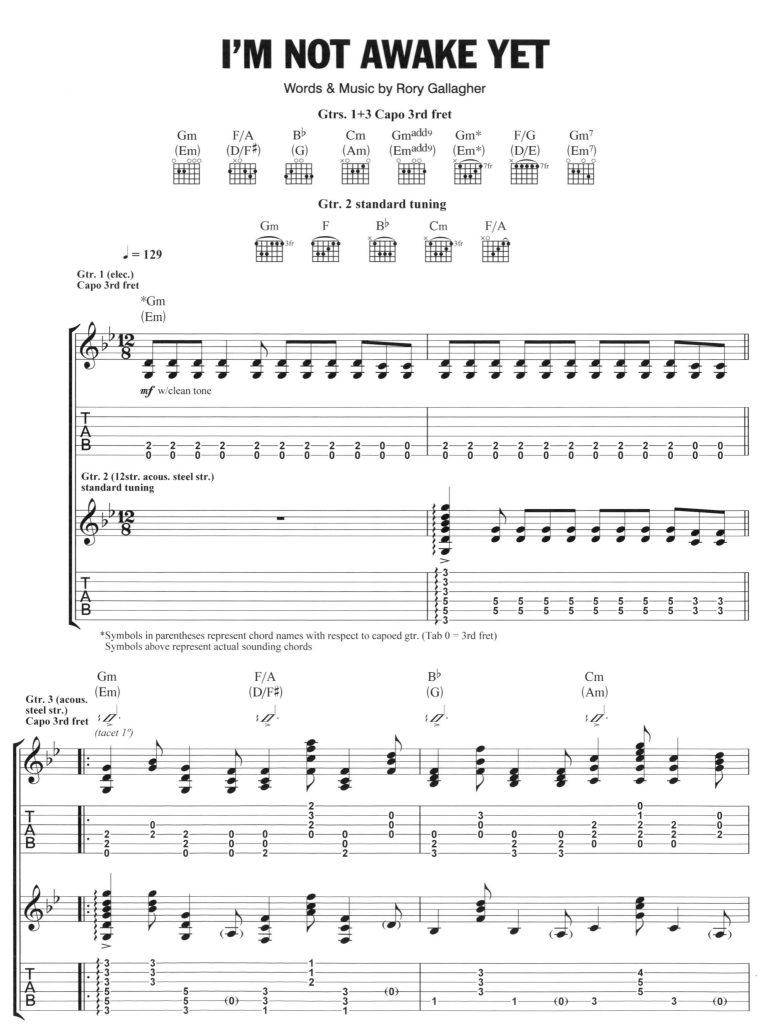

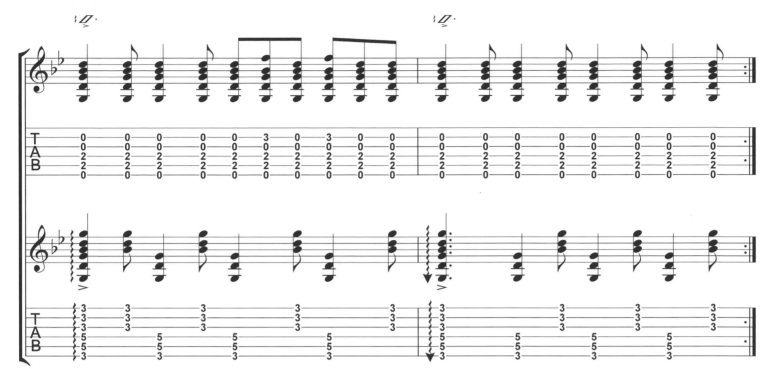

Verse

1. I'm____ not a - wake yet,____ I____ have - n't o - pened___ my
(2.) much____ can I take now____ be - fore I break in -
(3.) for - got my heart now____ and I trust - ed____ my

(end Gtr. 3 solo)

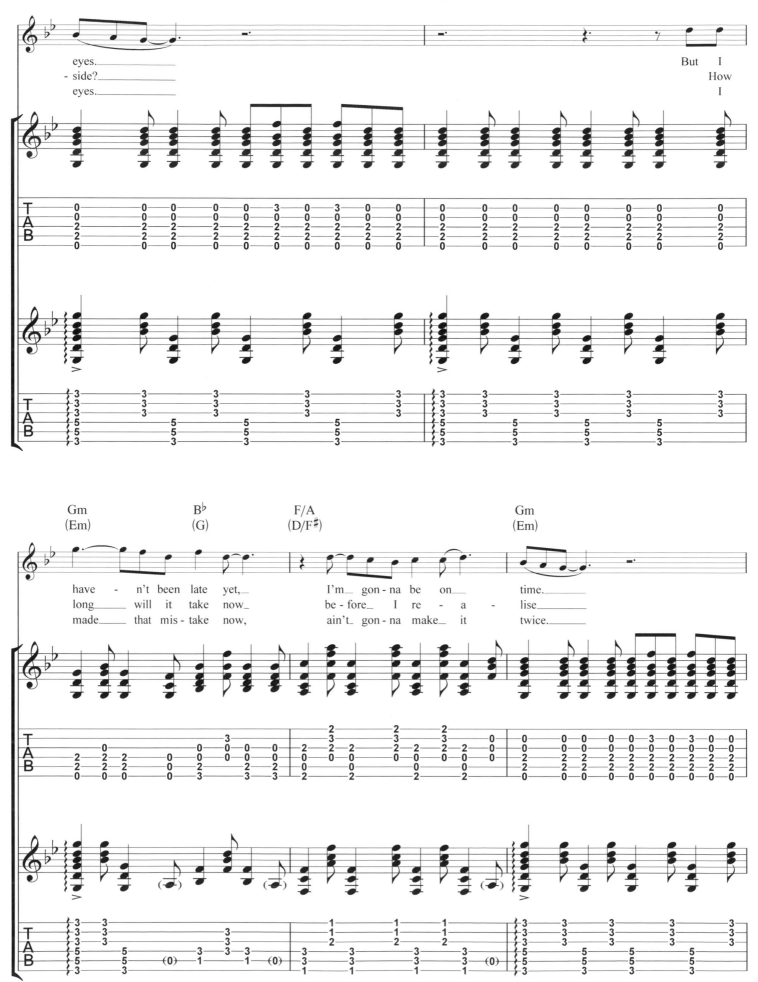

72

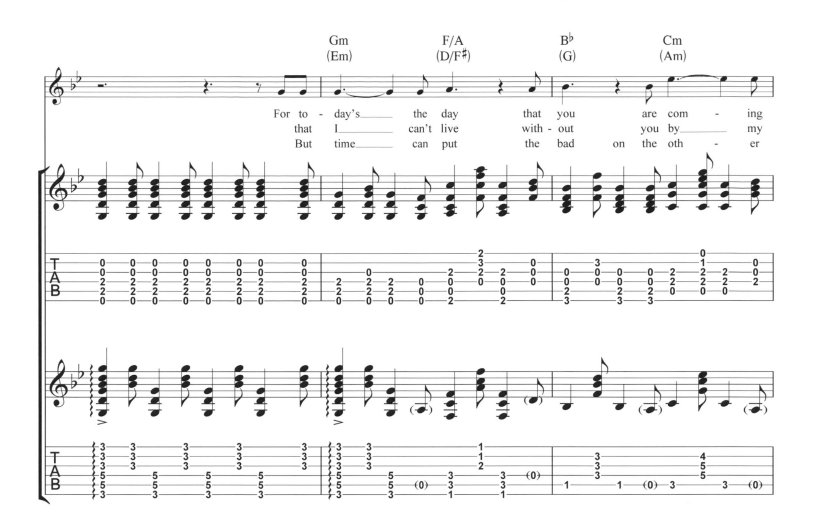

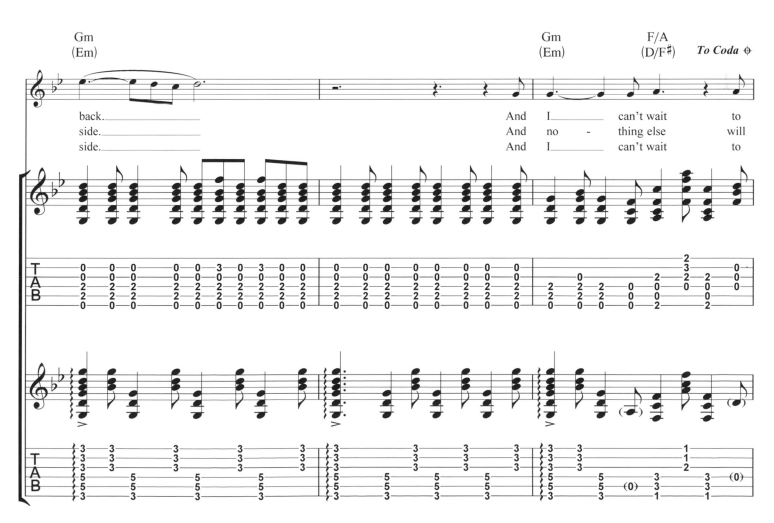

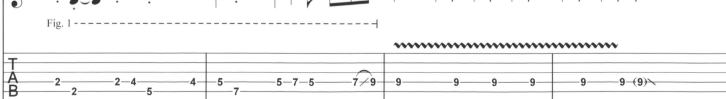

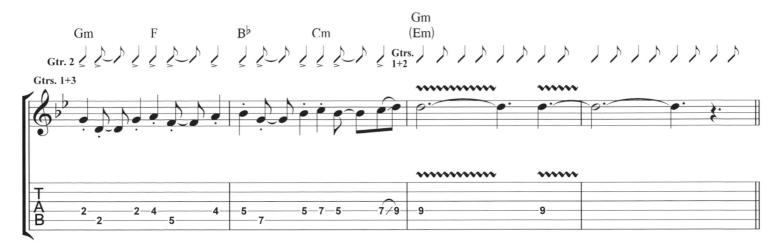

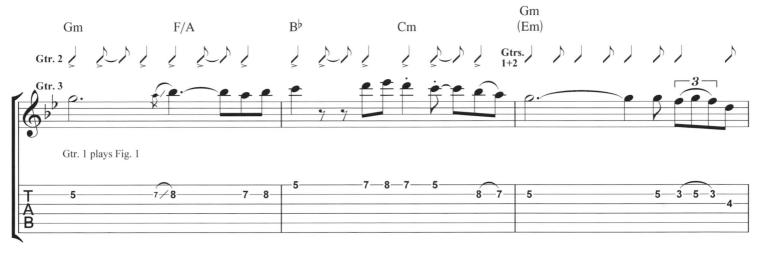

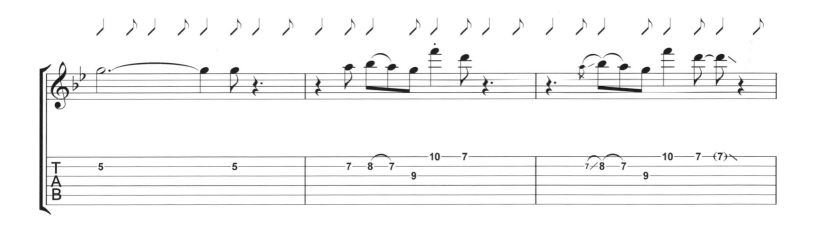

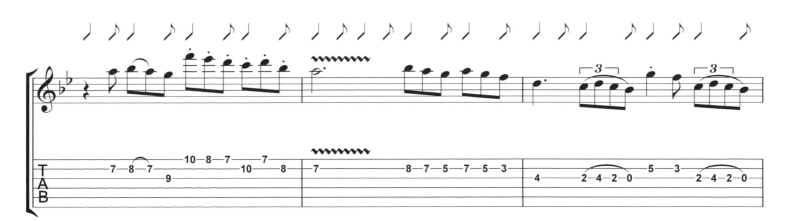

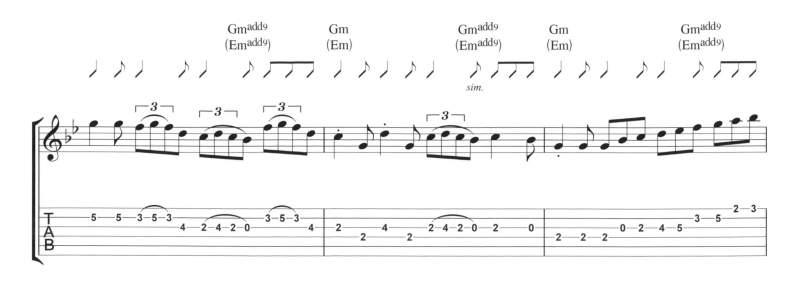

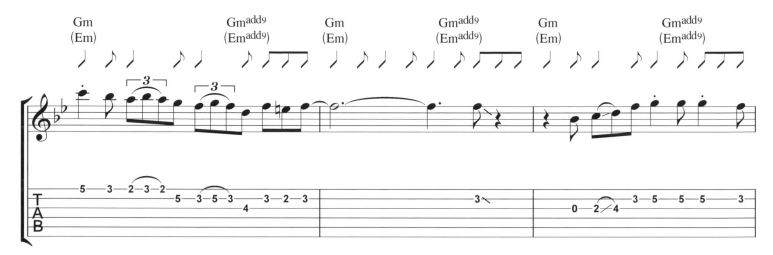

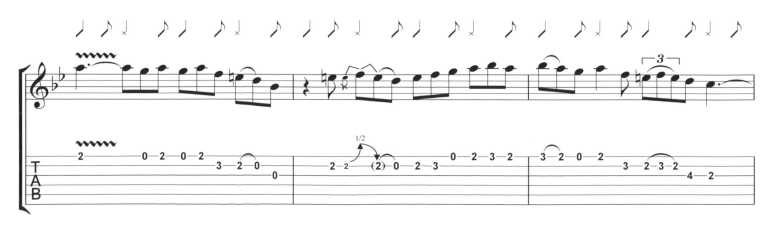

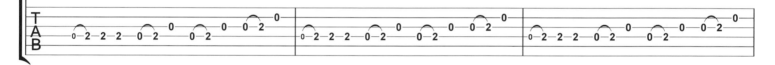

let ring…

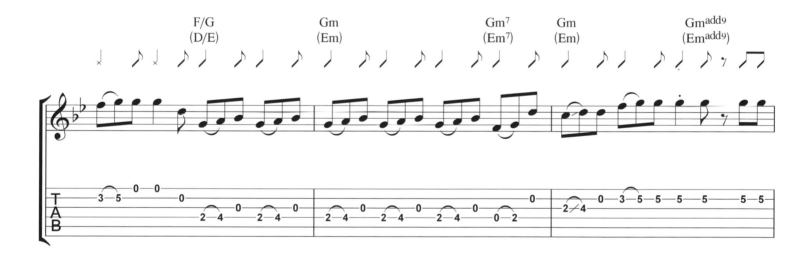

Gm*
(Em*)

F/G          Gm              Gm⁷      Gm              Gmadd9
(D/E)        (Em)            (Em⁷)    (Em)            (Emadd9)

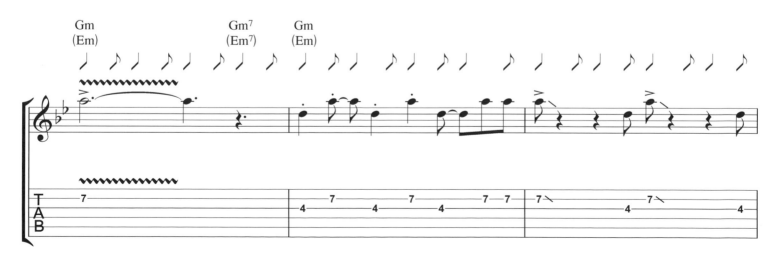

Gm           Gm⁷       Gm
(Em)         (Em⁷)     (Em)

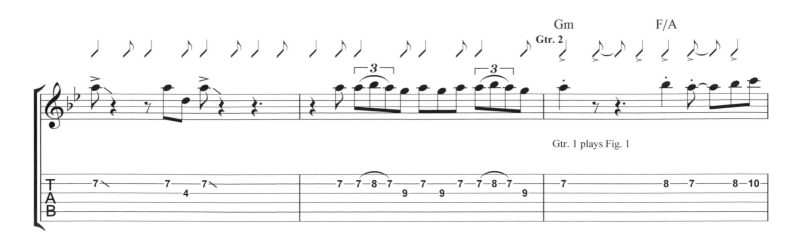

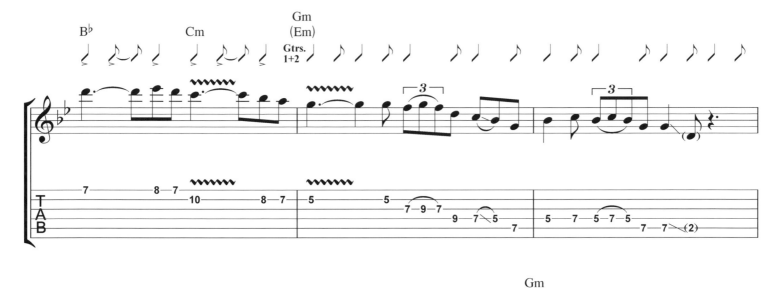

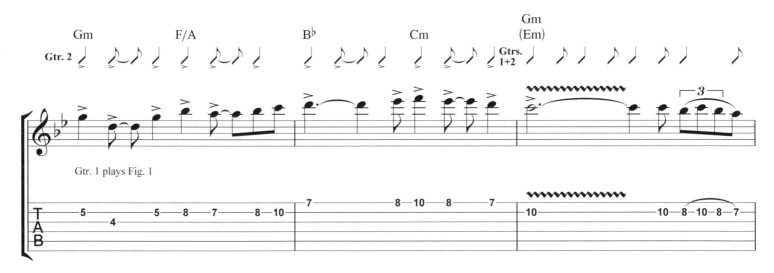

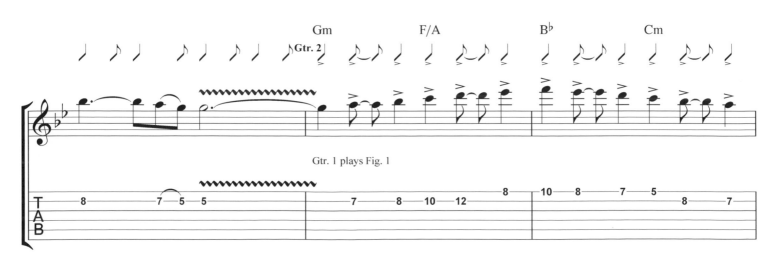

3. I

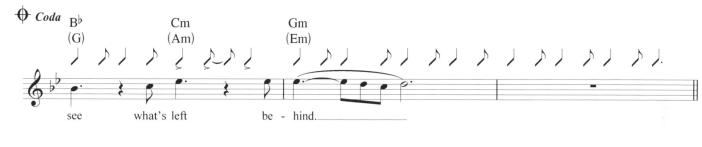

see    what's left    be - hind.

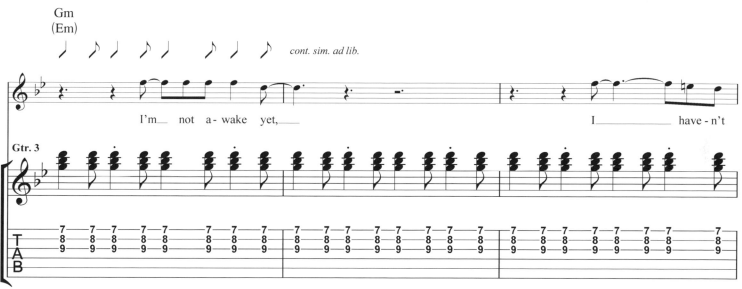

I'm    not a- wake    yet,    I_____ have - n't

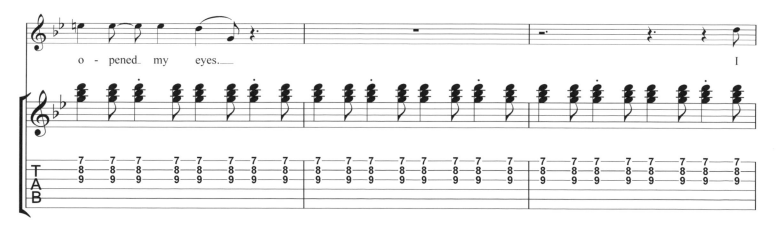

o - pened    my    eyes.____    I

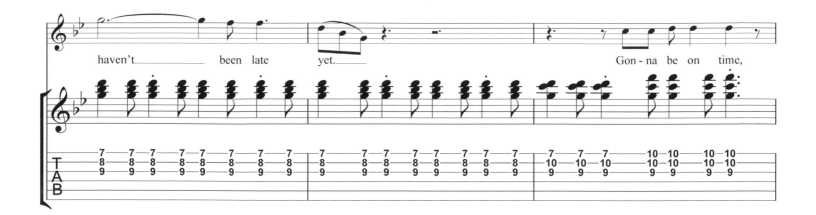

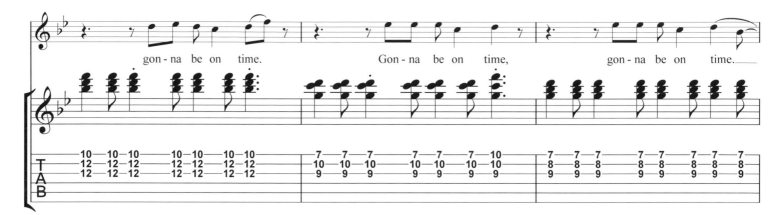

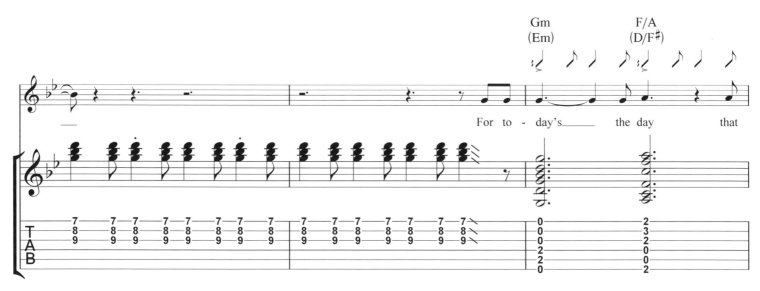

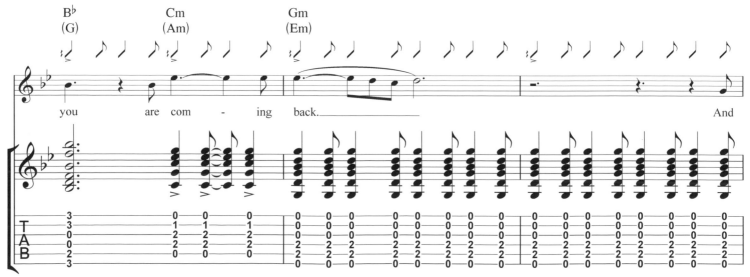

**Outro solo**

Gm
(Em)

*cont. sim ad lib.*

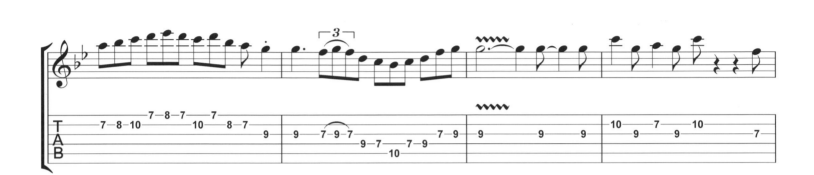

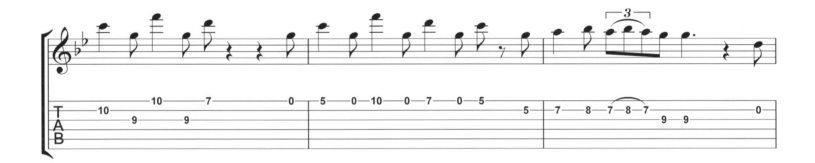

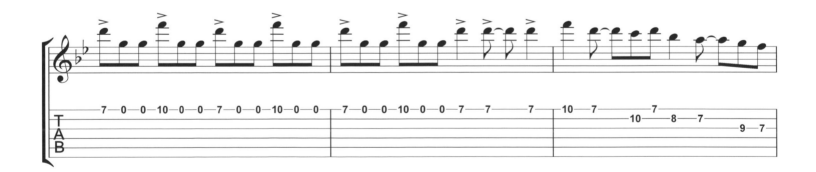

82

# I'M NOT SURPRISED

Words & Music by Rory Gallagher

**a tempo** (♩ = 116) (♫ = ♪♪³)

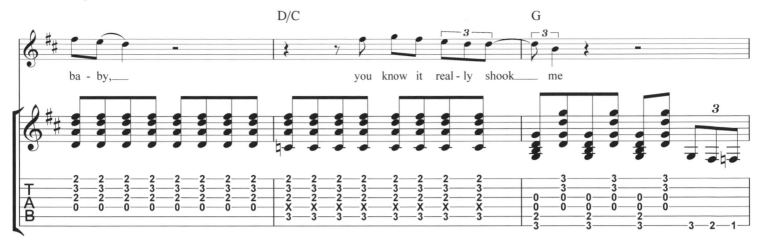

ba - by,____              you know it real - ly shook____ me

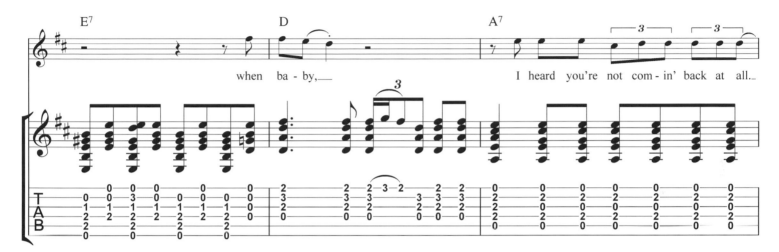

when ba - by,____              I heard you're not com - in' back at all.____

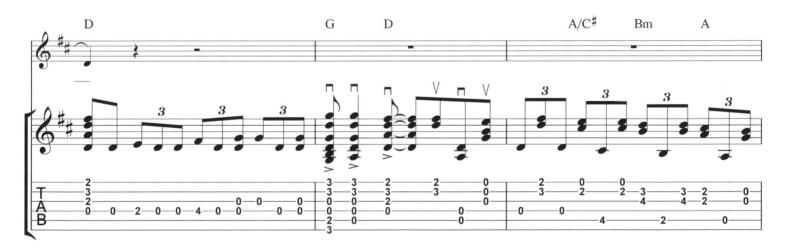

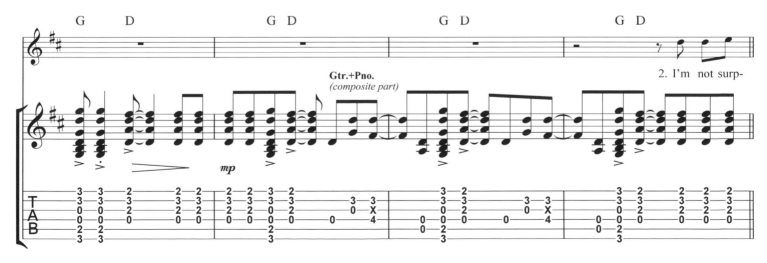

**Gtr.+Pno.**
*(composite part)*

2. I'm not surp-

**85**

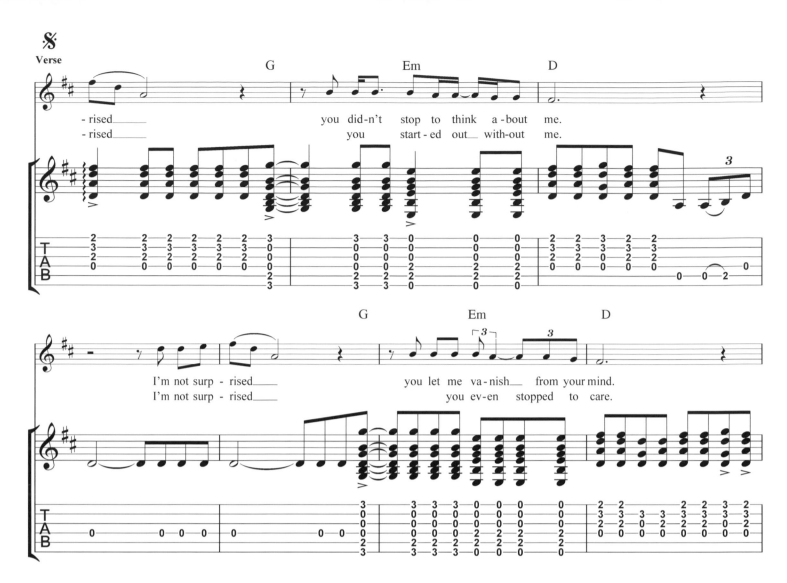

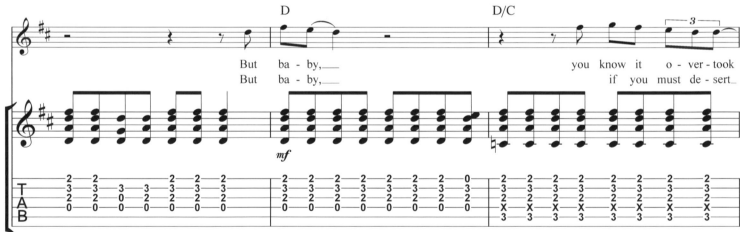

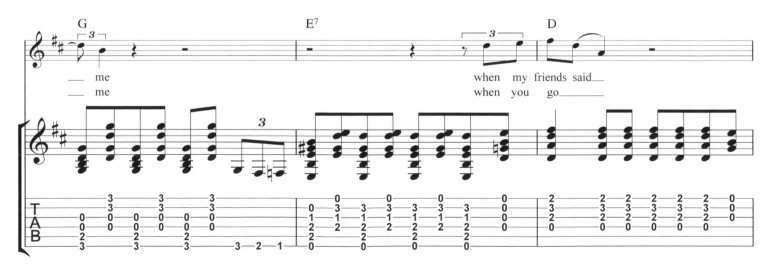

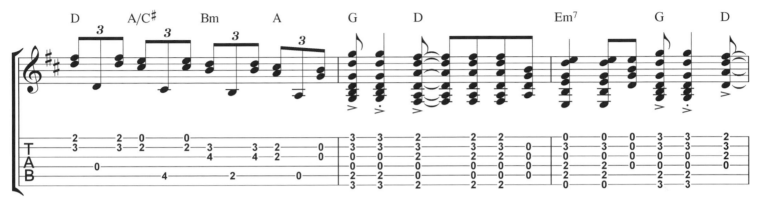

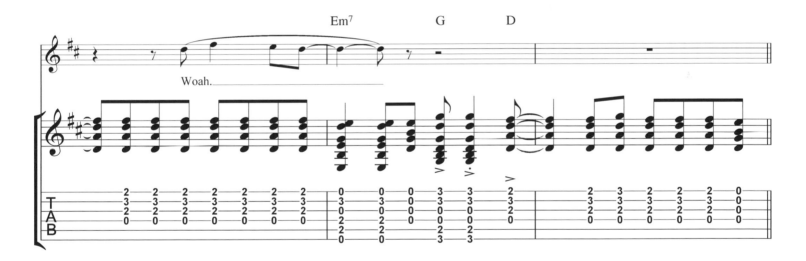

**Bridge**

Why must it be?_____

Why must it be?_____

**Solo**

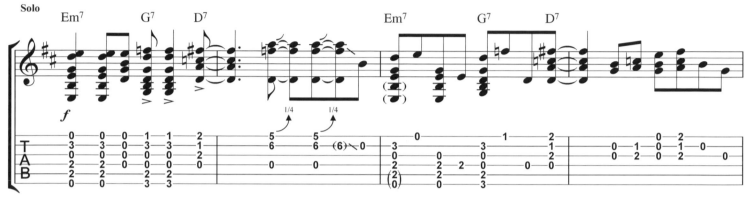

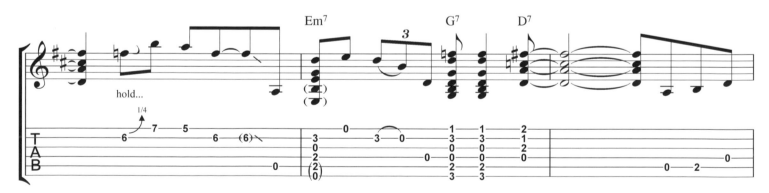

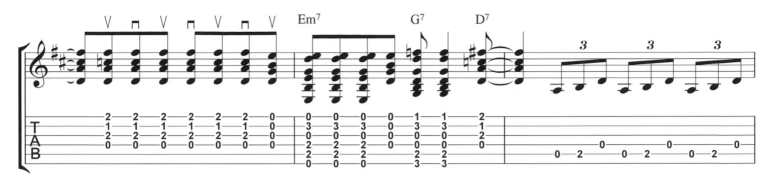

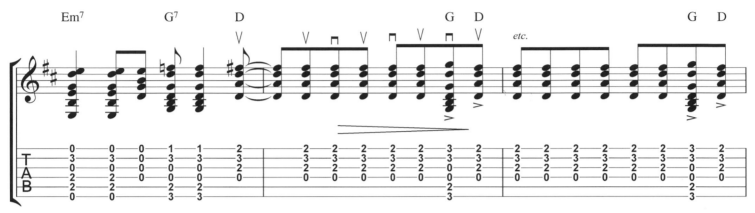

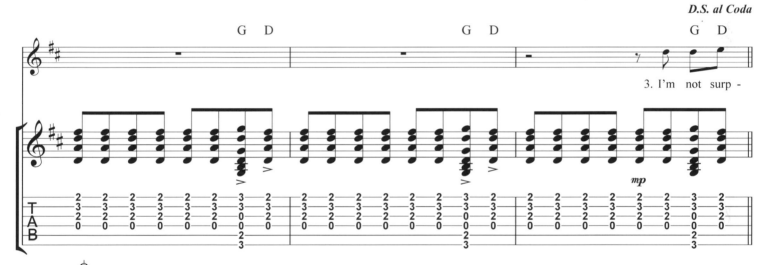

*D.S. al Coda*

3. I'm not surp -

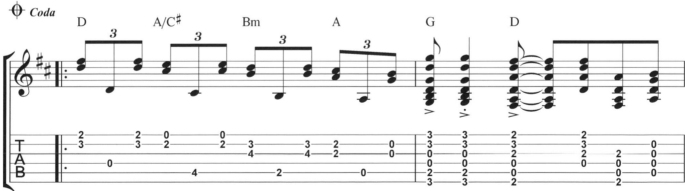

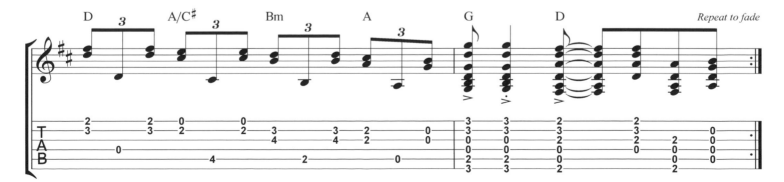

*Repeat to fade*

# JUST THE SMILE

Words & Music by Rory Gallagher

1. Just the

**Verse**

smile that is spread-ing all o - ver her face___ could warm up the room___ and set fire___ to the place.
(2.) fog is___ cling-ing all o - ver the town, put one foot in front then you just___ might fall down___

**1.**

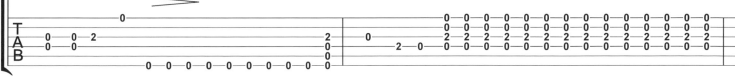

Yes it could, you know it could.
on the ground,

**2.**

2. Now the she's in town.

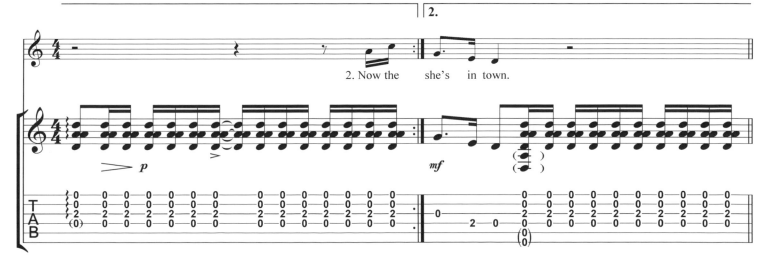

Solo

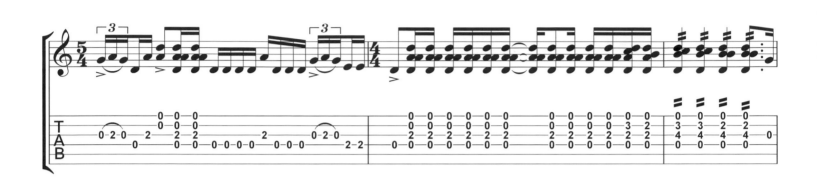

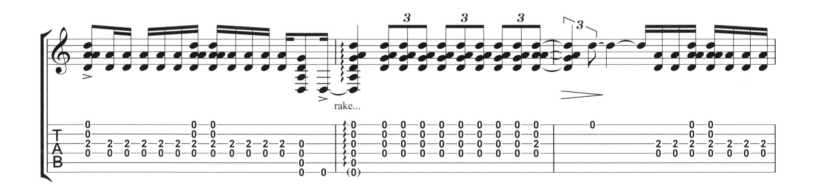

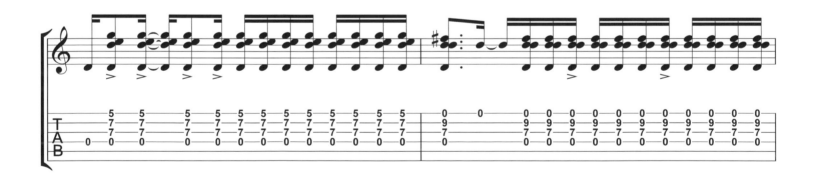

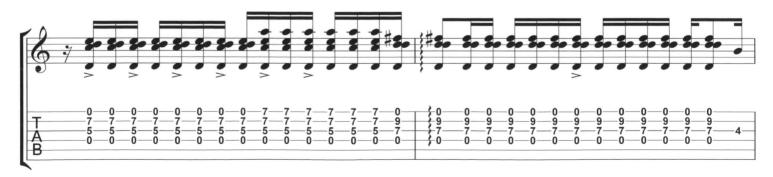

92

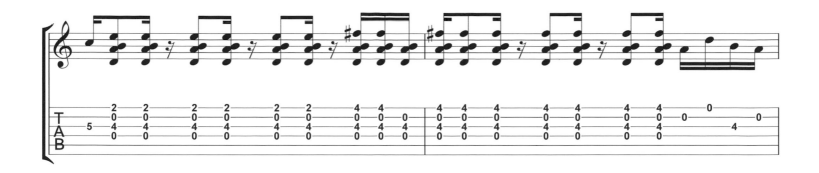

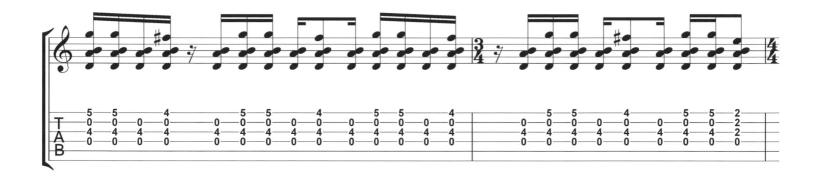

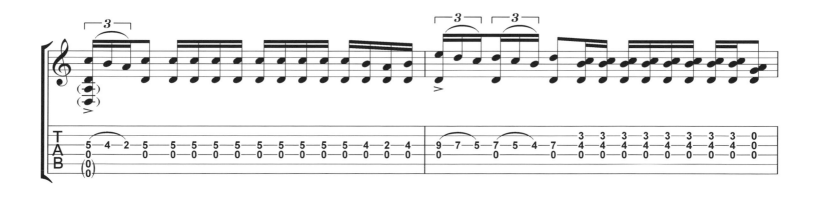

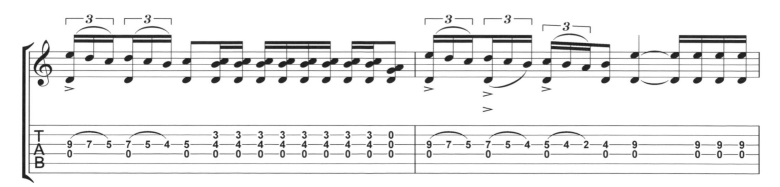

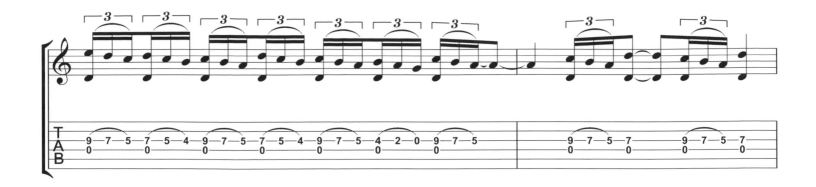

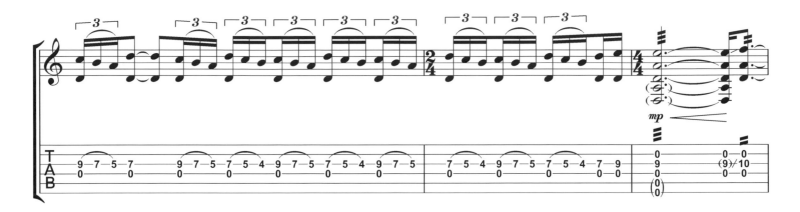

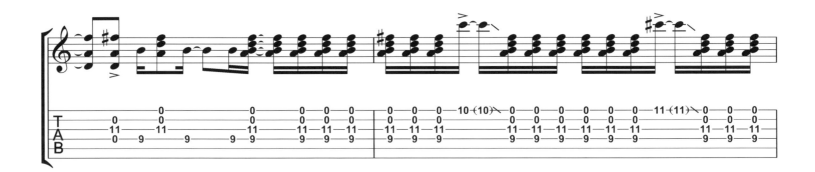

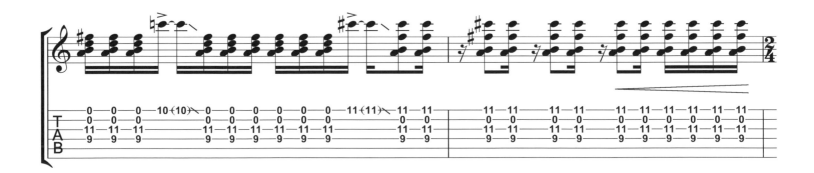

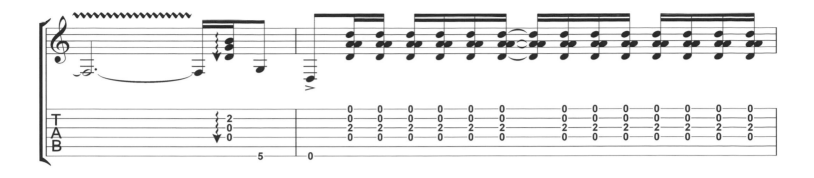

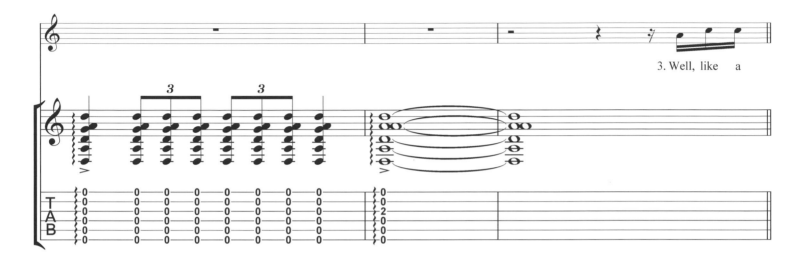

3. Well, like    a

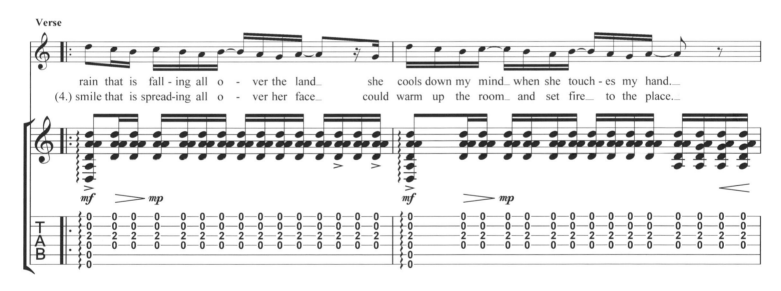

**Verse**

rain that is fall - ing all o - ver the land___ she cools down my mind___ when she touch - es my hand.___
(4.) smile that is spread-ing all o - ver her face___ could warm up the room___ and set fire___ to the place.___

*mf*   *mp*   *mf*   *mp*

1.

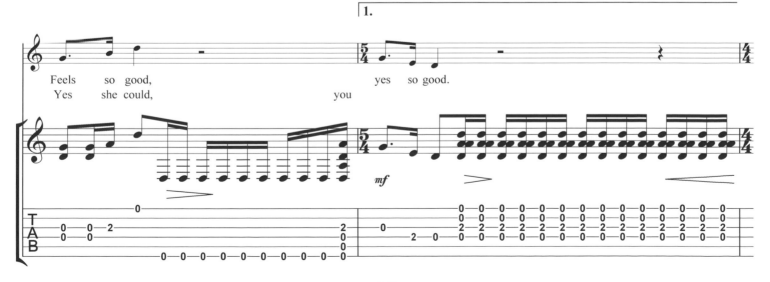

Feels    so good,                    yes    so good.
Yes    she could,                    you

*mf*

4. With just the    know    it could.

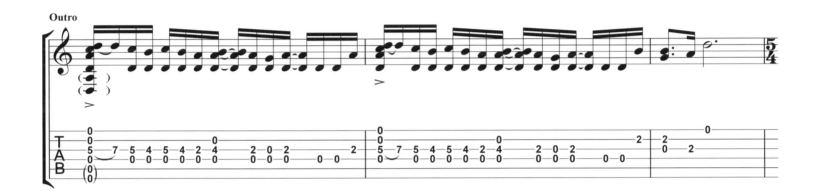

**Outro**

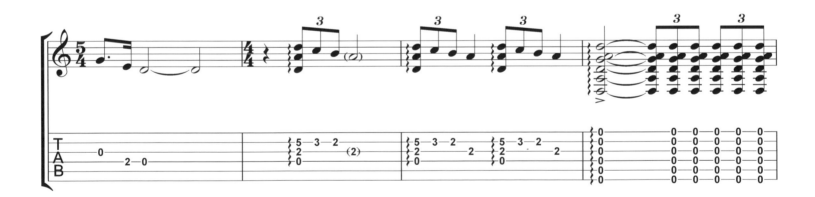

*w/ad lib. percussion to fade*

# NOTHIN' BUT THE DEVIL

Words & Music by Rory Gallagher

y'ain't back 'til late at night.___   That's no-thing but the dev-il   make you treat me the way you do.

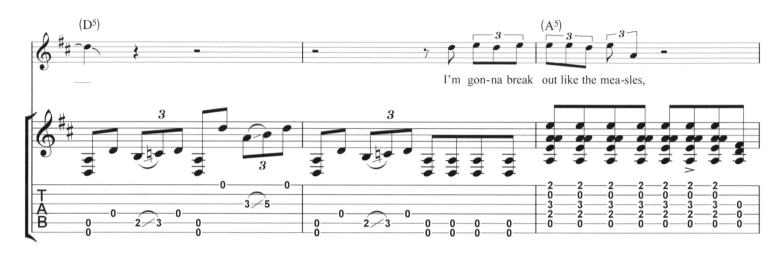

I'm gon-na break out like the mea-sles,

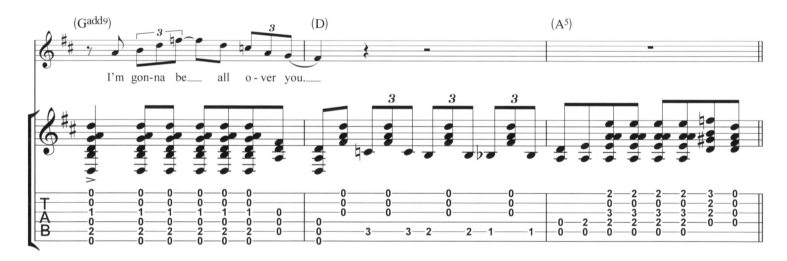

I'm gon-na be___ all o-ver you.___

**Verse**

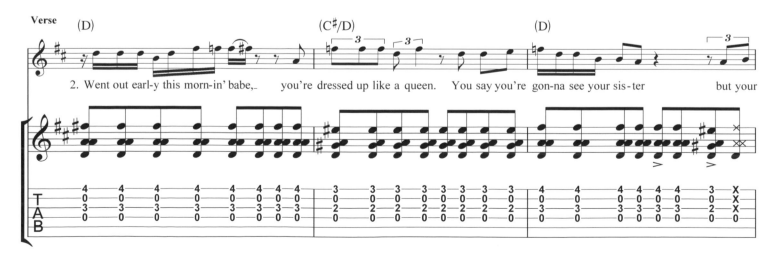

2. Went out earl-y this morn-in' babe,___ you're dressed up like a queen.   You say you're gon-na see your sis-ter   but your

sis-ter you've ne-ver seen.___ That's no-thing but the de-vil,___ make you treat me the way you do.

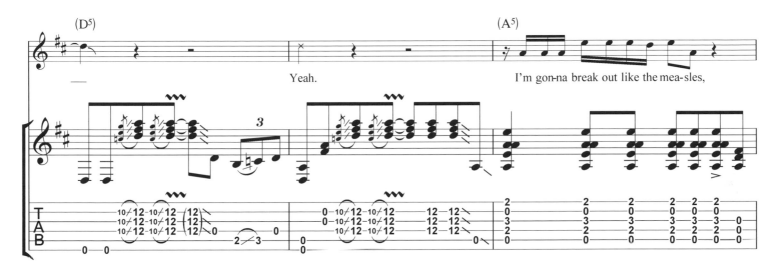

Yeah. I'm gon-na break out like the mea-sles,

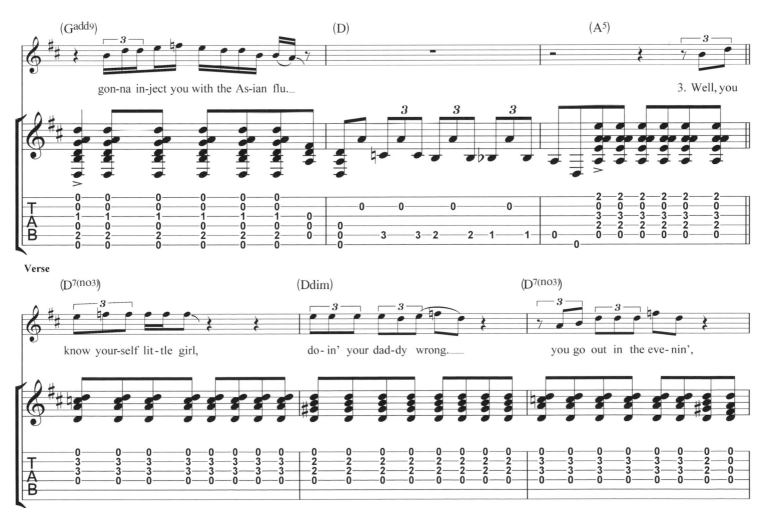

gon-na in-ject you with the As-ian flu.___ 3. Well, you

know your-self lit-tle girl, do-in' your dad-dy wrong.___ you go out in the eve-nin',

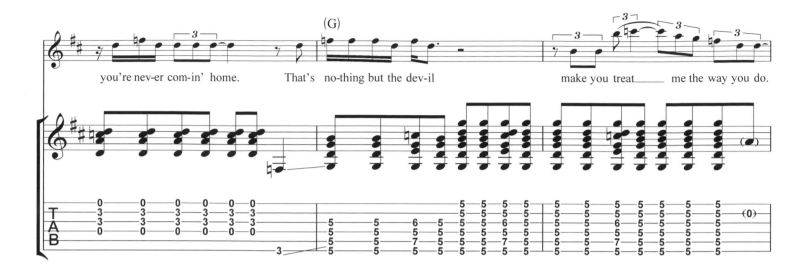

you're nev-er com-in' home.   That's no-thing but the dev-il   make you treat___ me the way you do.

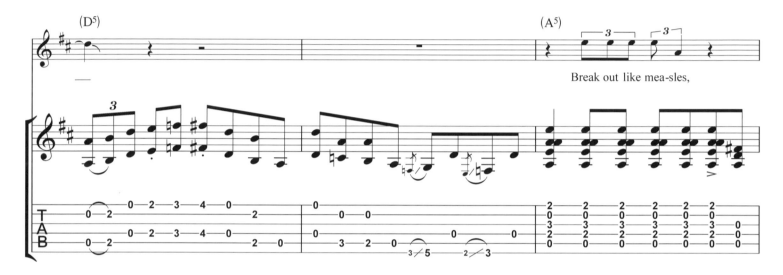

Break out like mea-sles,

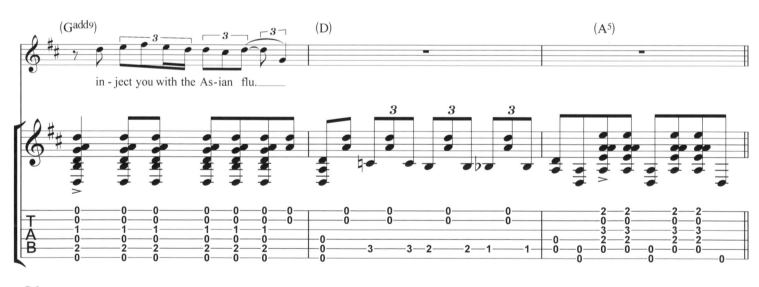

in - ject you with the As-ian flu.___

**Solo**

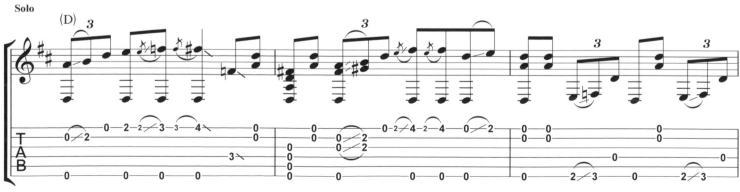

100

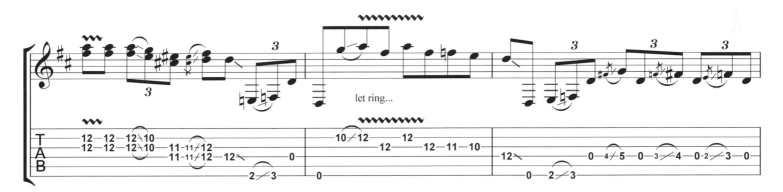

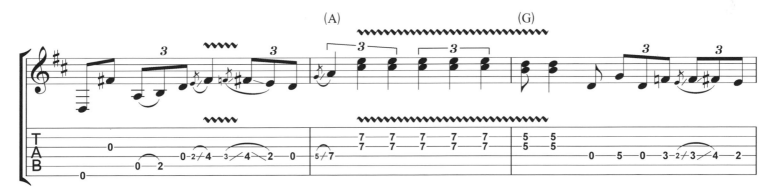

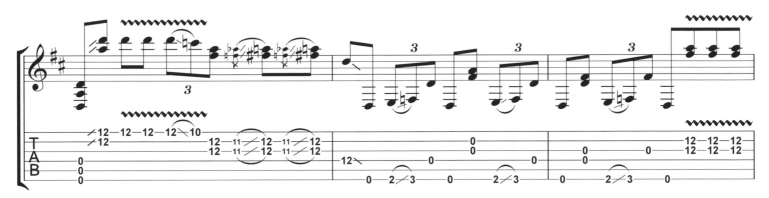

4. Well, you know your-

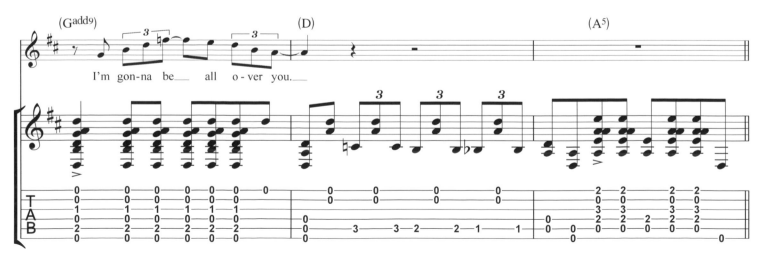

**Outro**

Ooh,_____ ooh._____

Ooh,_____ ooh.

I'm gon-na break out like the mea-sles,

gon-na be____ all o-ver you.____

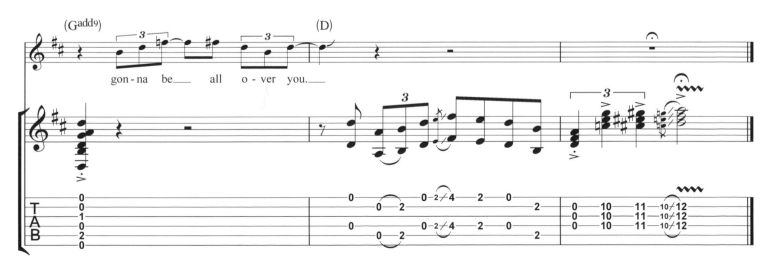

# OUT OF MY MIND

Words & Music by Rory Gallagher

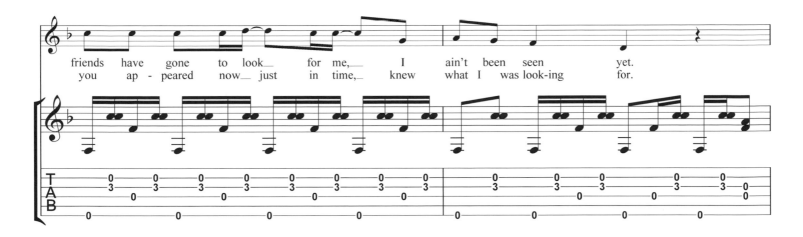

friends have gone to look for me, I ain't been seen yet.
you ap - peared now just in time, I knew what I was look-ing for.

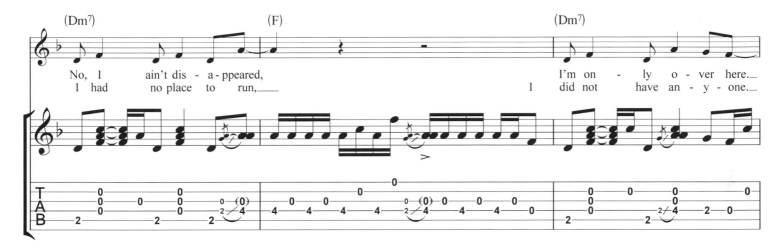

(Dm⁷)　(F)　(Dm⁷)

No, I ain't dis - a - ppeared, I'm on - ly o - ver here.
I had no place to run, I did not have an - y - one.

**1.**

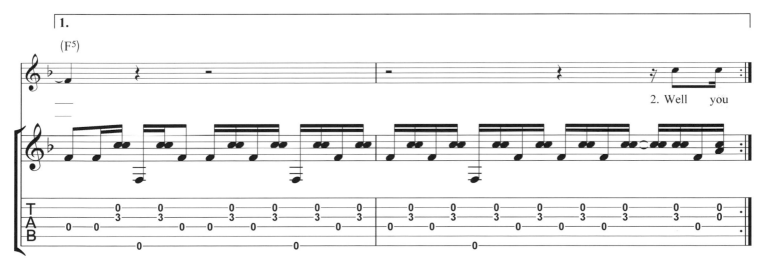

(F⁵)

2. Well you

**2.**

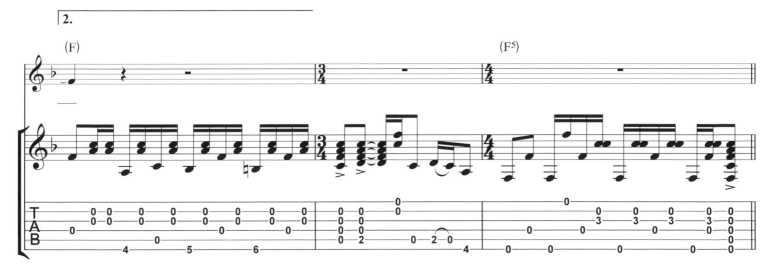

(F)　(F⁵)

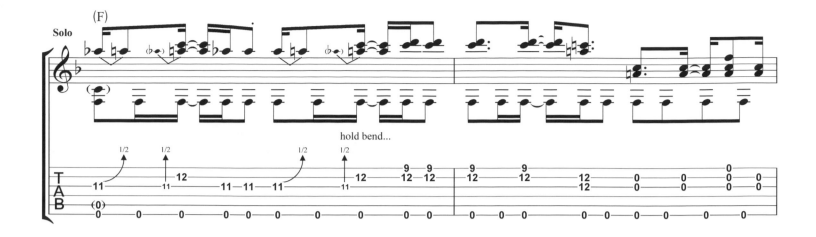

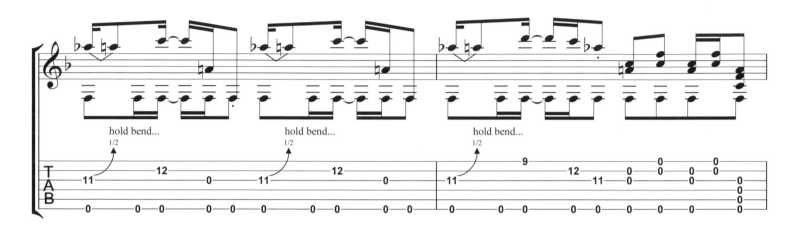

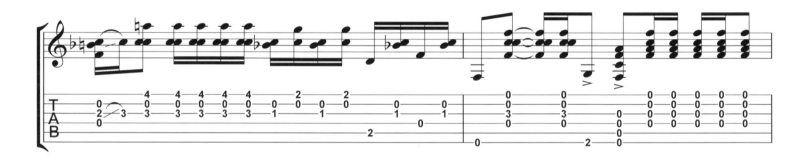

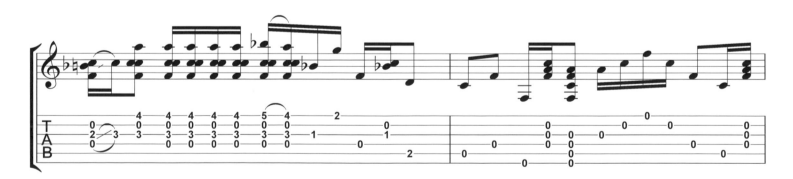

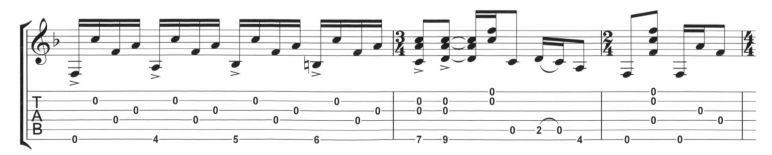

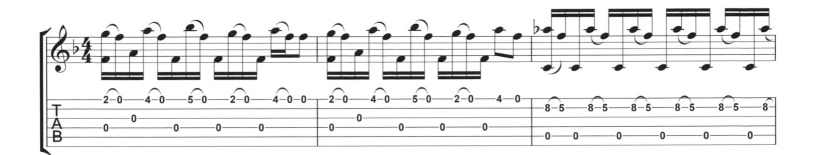

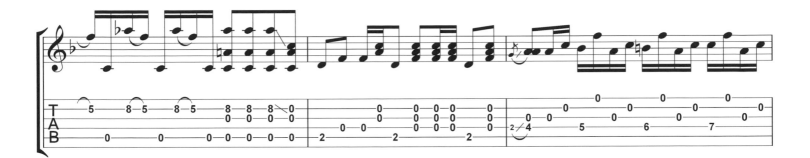

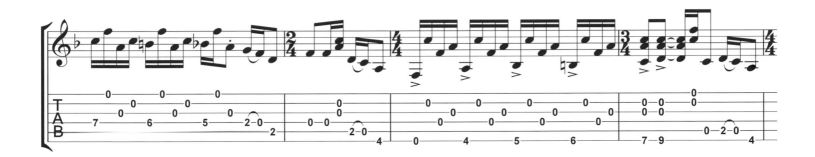

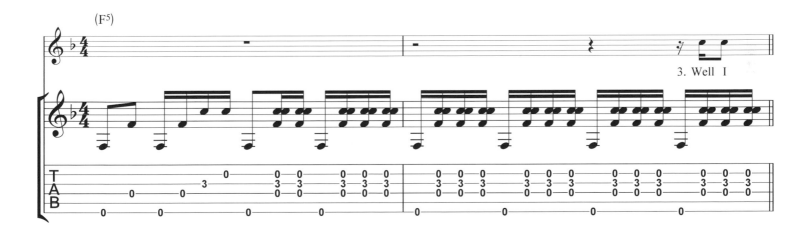

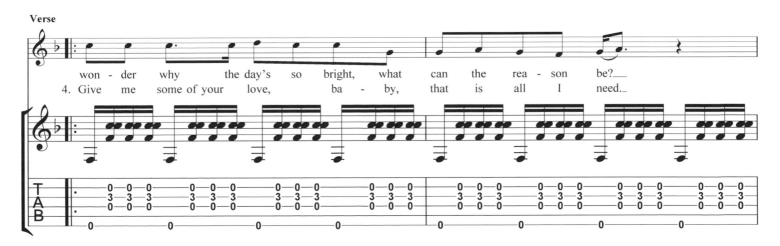

won - der   why      the day's  so   bright,  what    can    the    rea - son    be?___
4. Give  me    some of your    love,      ba  -  by,   that    is    all    I     need.__

You light up the dark-est night like a pearl out of the sea.
Tell me up what it's all a-bout, tell me what you see.

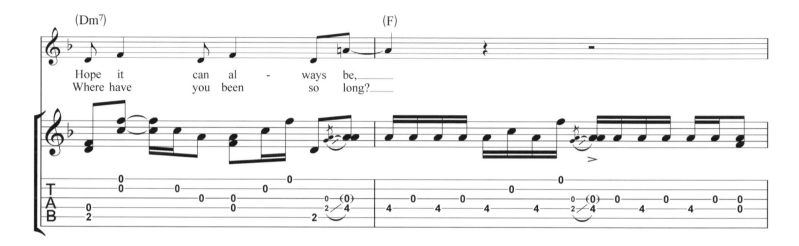

(Dm7)                                    (F)

Hope it can al - ways be,
Where have you been so long?

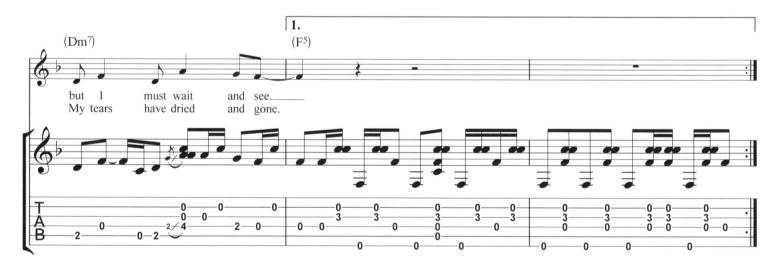

**1.**

(Dm7)                          (F5)

but I must wait and see.
My tears have dried and gone.

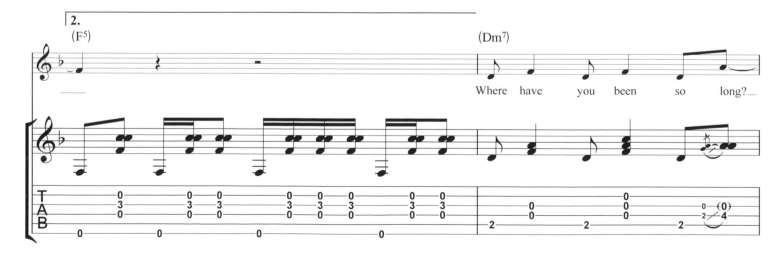

**2.**

(F5)                                        (Dm7)

Where have you been so long?

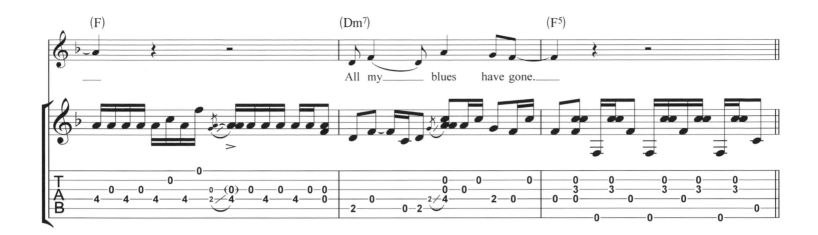

All my_____ blues have gone._____

**Solo**

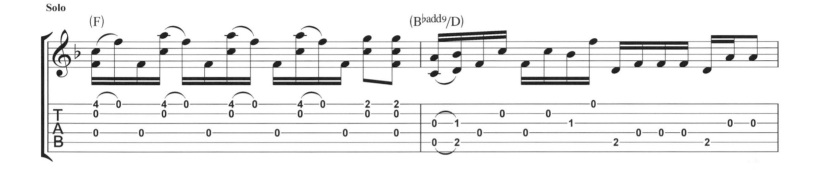

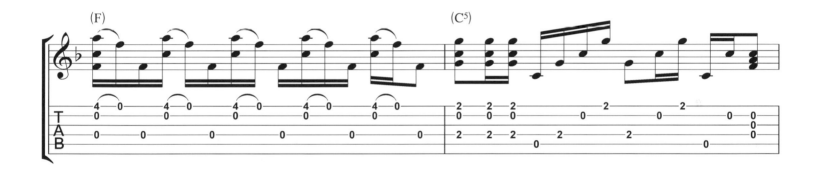

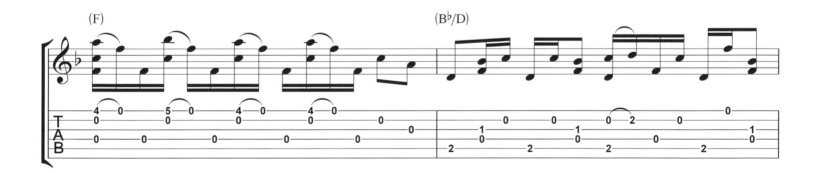

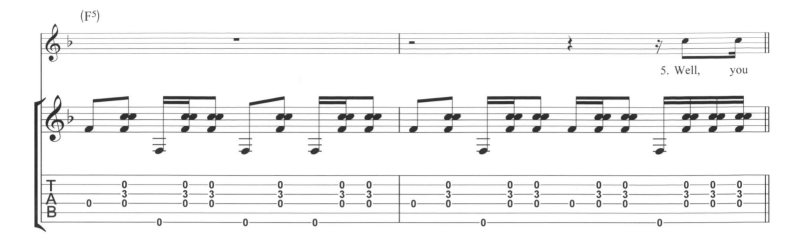

(F⁵)

5. Well, you

**Verse**

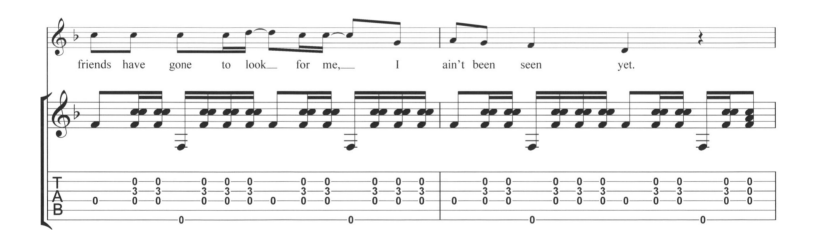

took me out of my mind, babe, you took me out of my head. My

friends have gone to look for me, I ain't been seen yet.

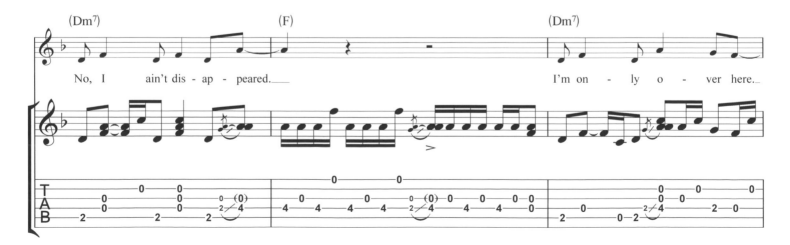

(Dm⁷)                    (F)                    (Dm⁷)

No, I ain't dis - ap - peared. I'm on - ly o - ver here.

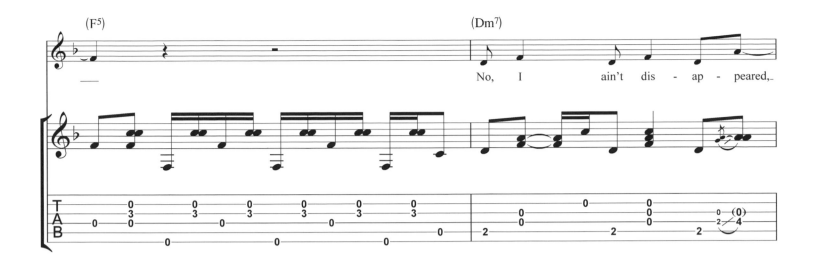

No, I         ain't dis - ap - peared,

I'm on - ly o - ver here.____

# PISTOL SLAPPER BLUES (LIVE)

Words & Music by Fulton Allen

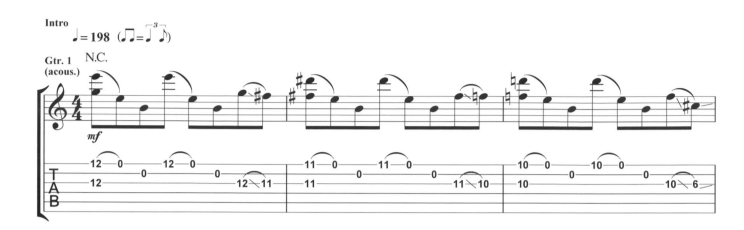

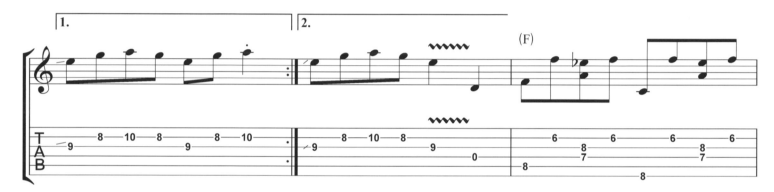

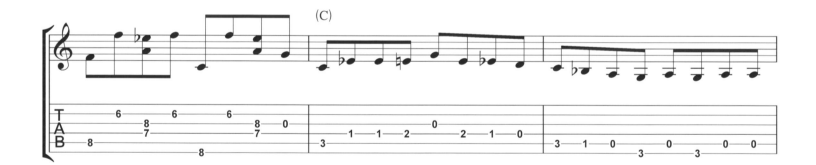

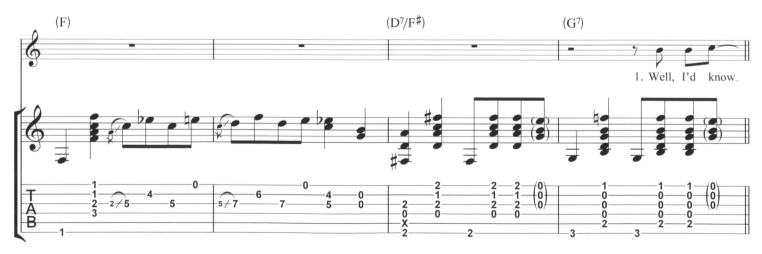

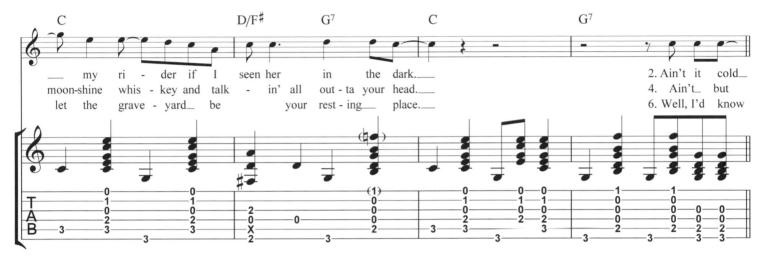

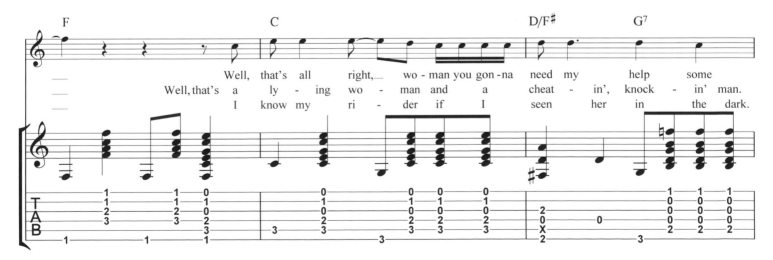

113

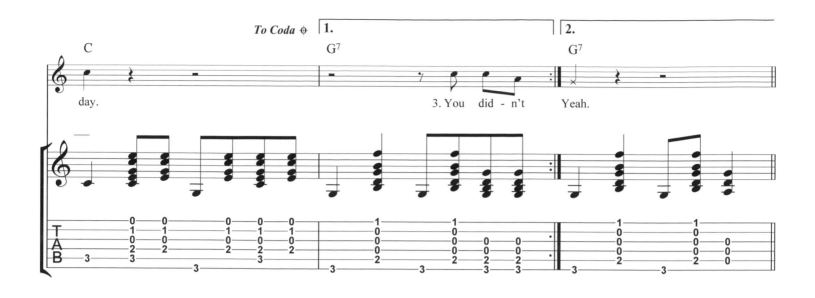

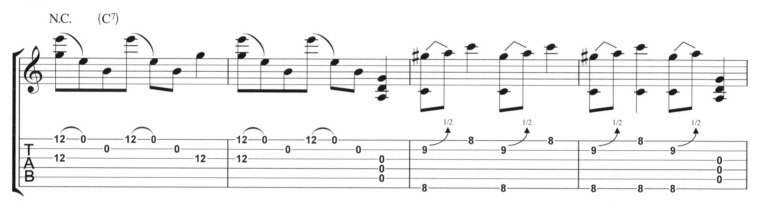

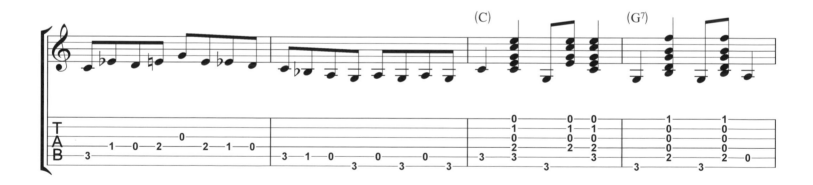

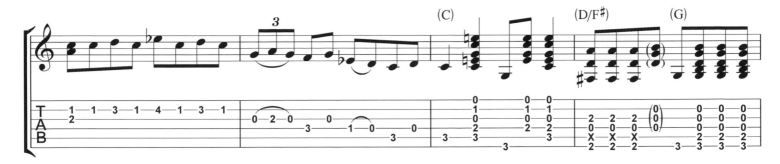

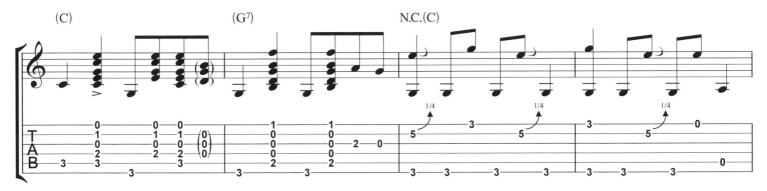

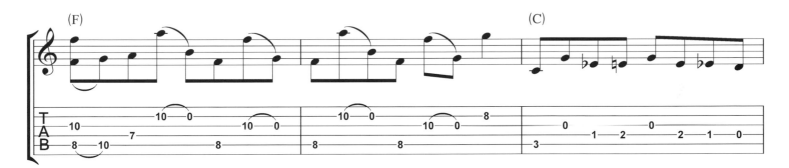

D.S. al Coda

5. Well, I feel

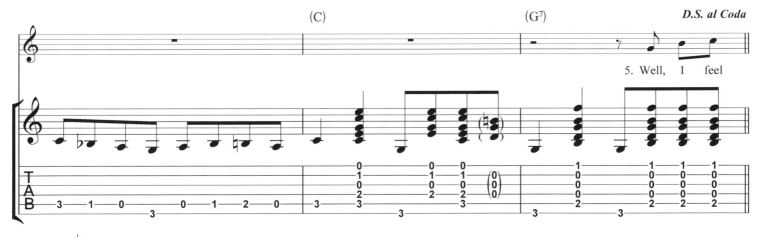

Coda

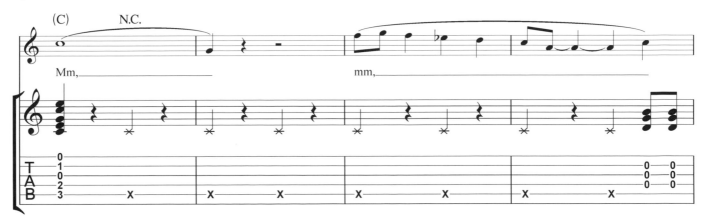

Mm,

mm,

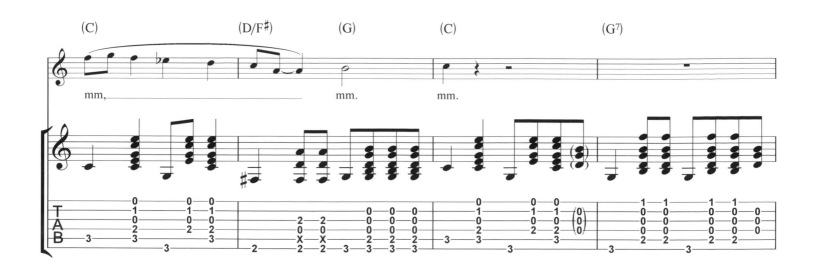

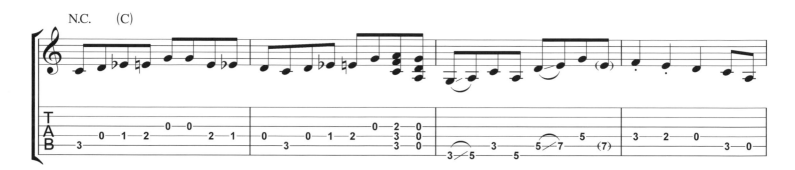

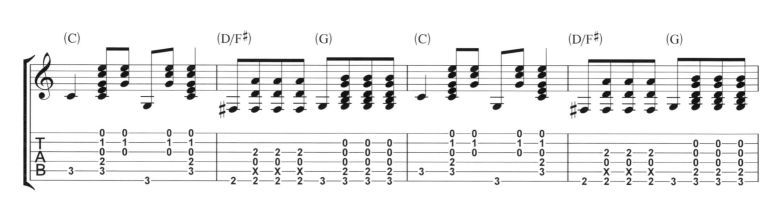

**Slowly, freely**

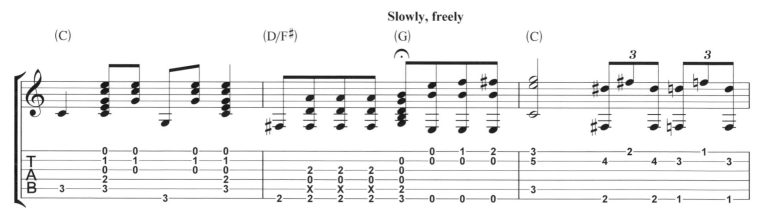

# UNMILITARY TWO-STEP

Music by Rory Gallagher

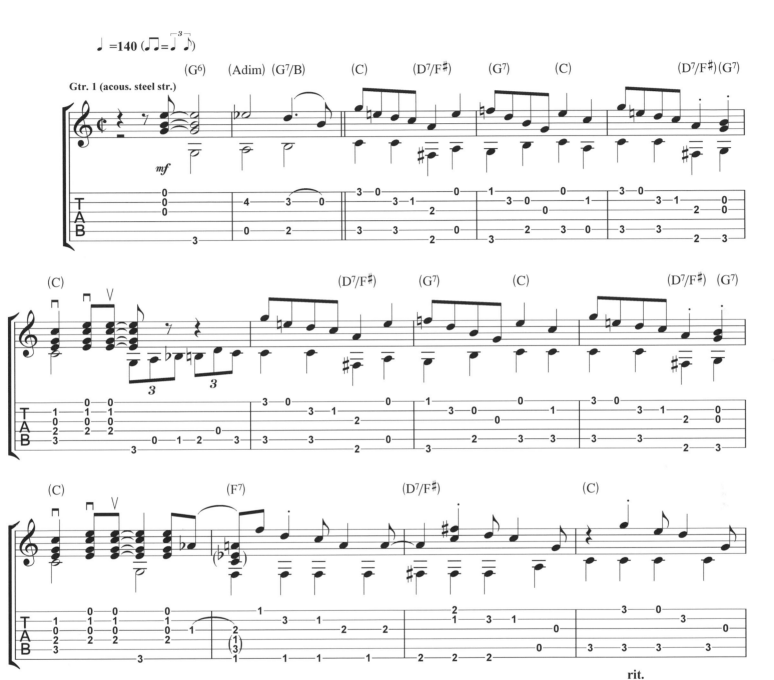

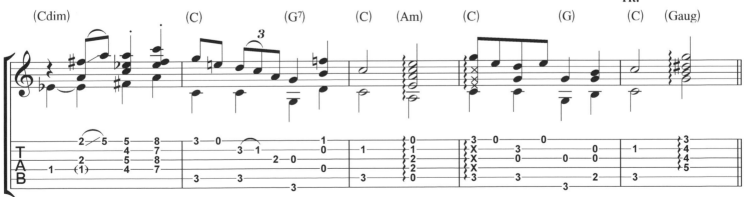

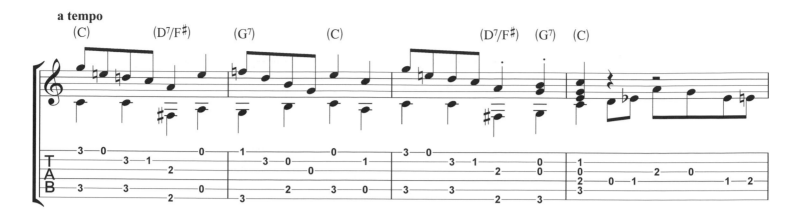

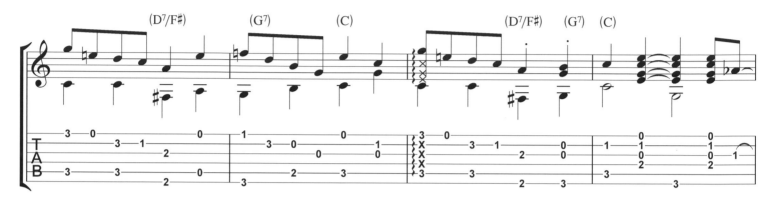

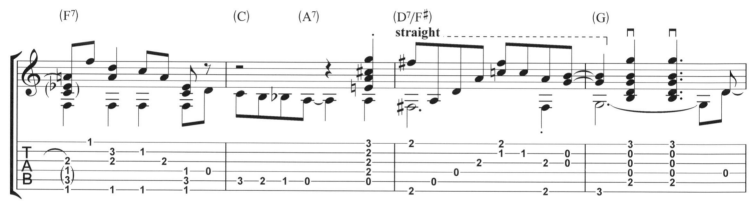

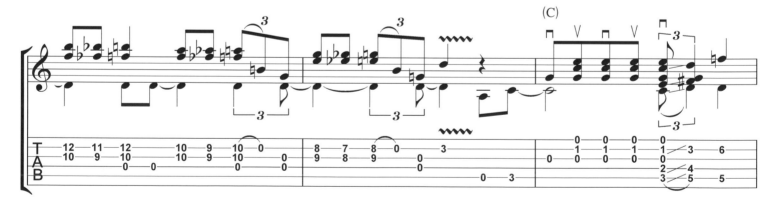

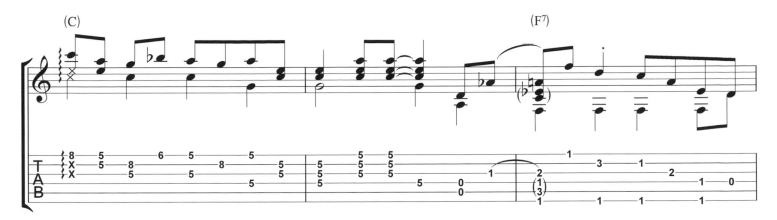

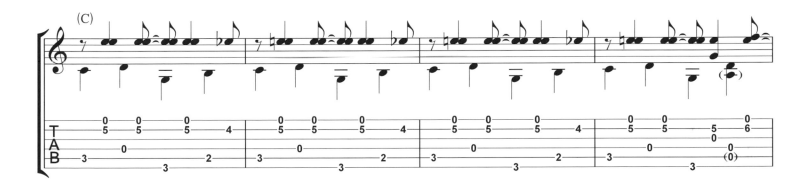

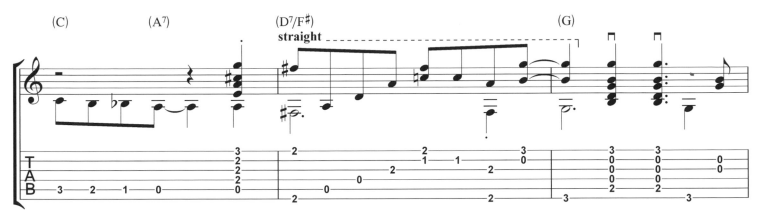

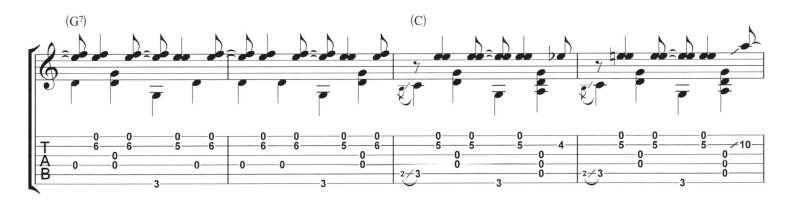

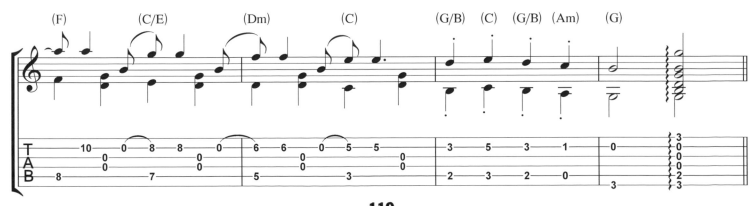

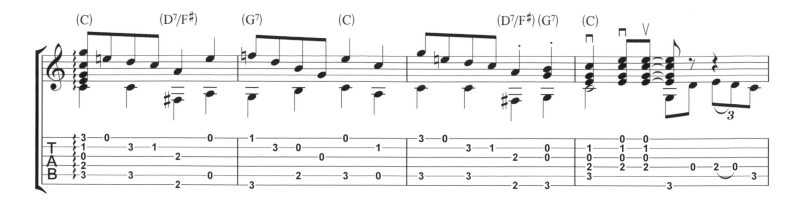

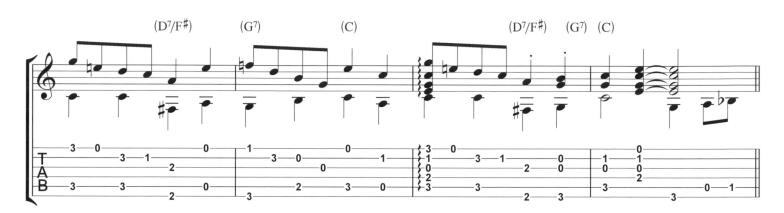

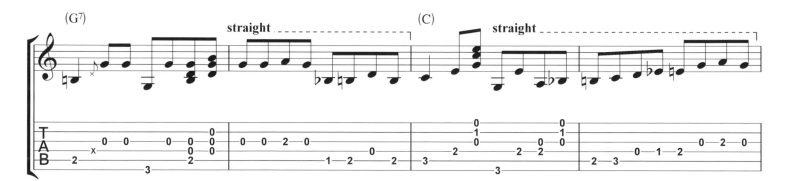

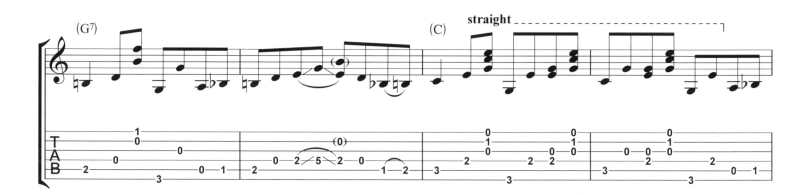

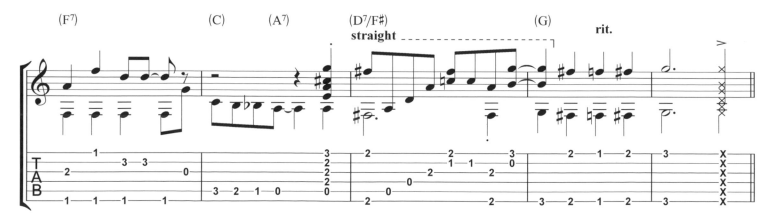

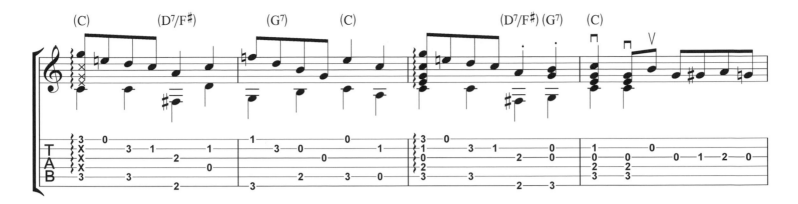

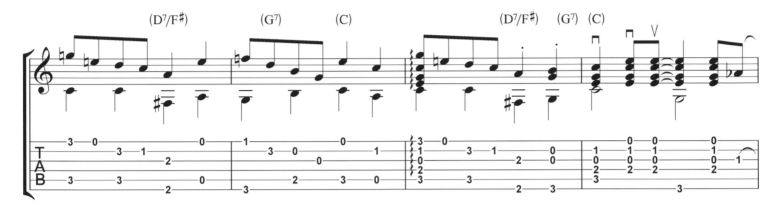

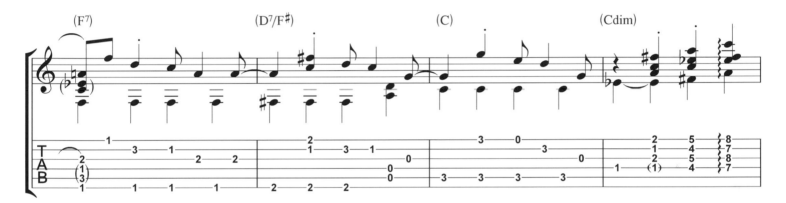

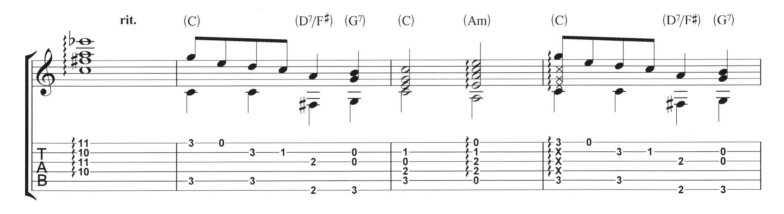

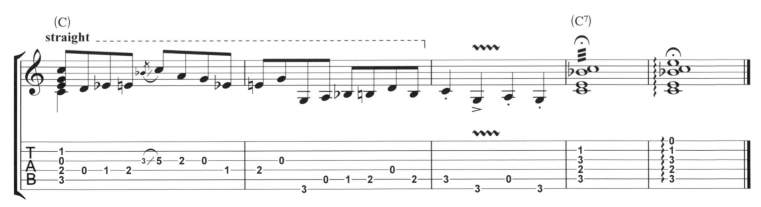

# SEVEN DAYS

Words & Music by Rory Gallagher

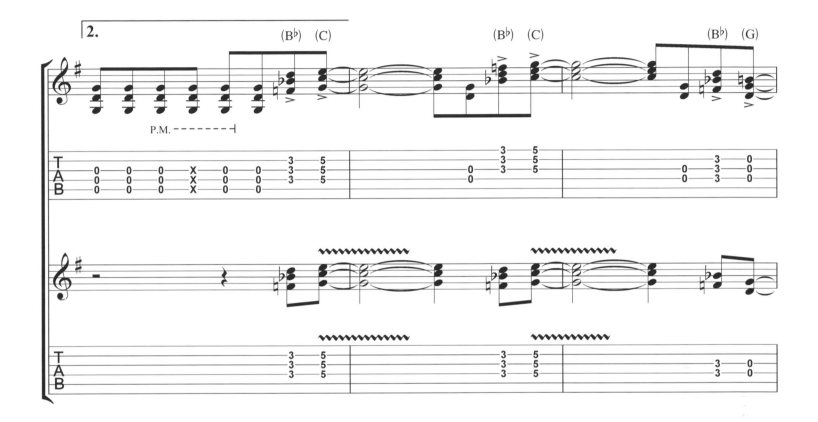

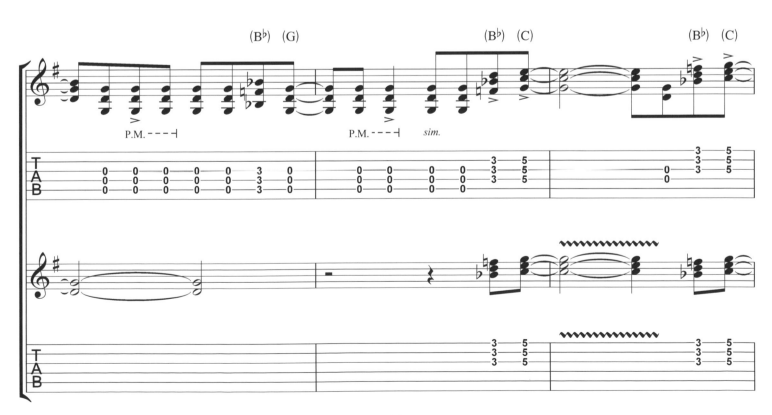

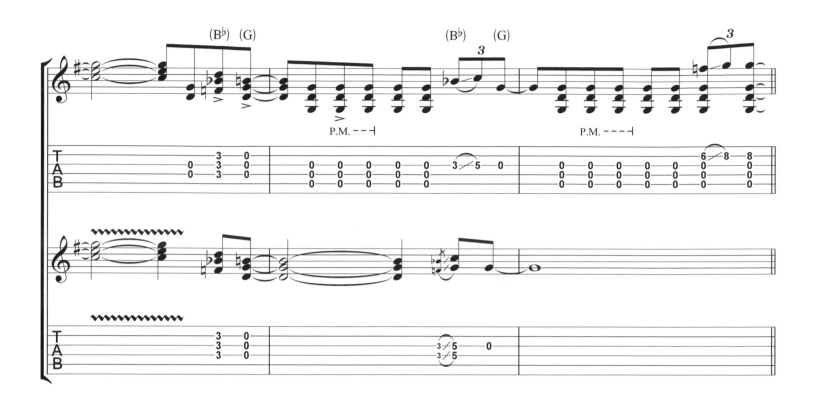

**Verse**

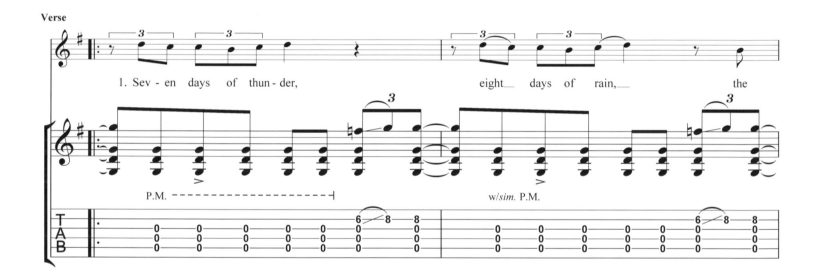

1. Sev - en days of thun - der,           eight  days  of  rain,           the

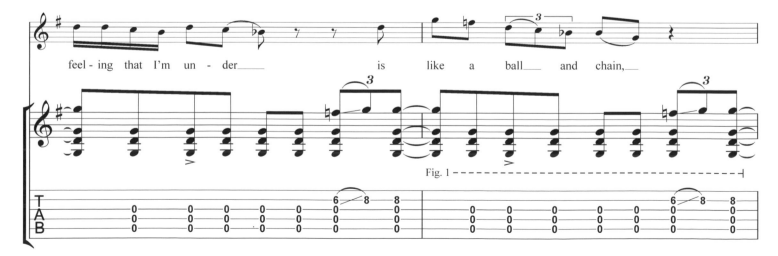

feel - ing that I'm un - der           is    like   a   ball    and   chain,

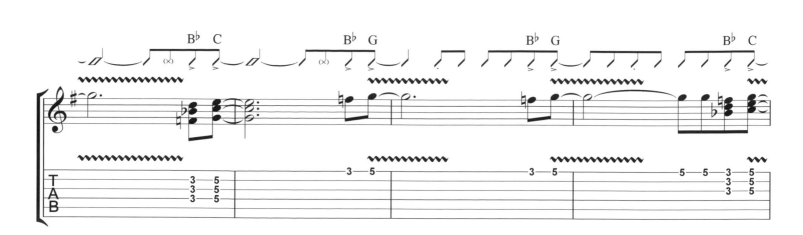

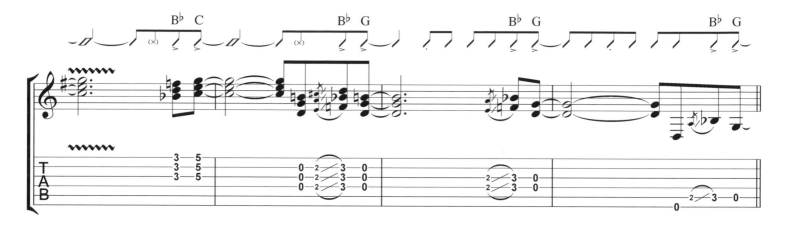

**Verse**

3. And if they catch me,___ they put me in the chair,___ you can sit be-side__ me, there's

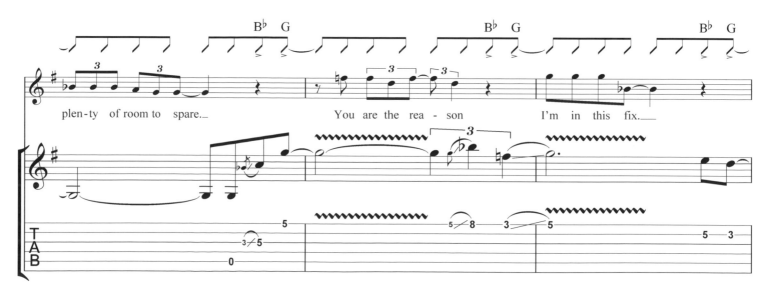

plen-ty of room to spare.___ You are the rea - son I'm in this fix.___

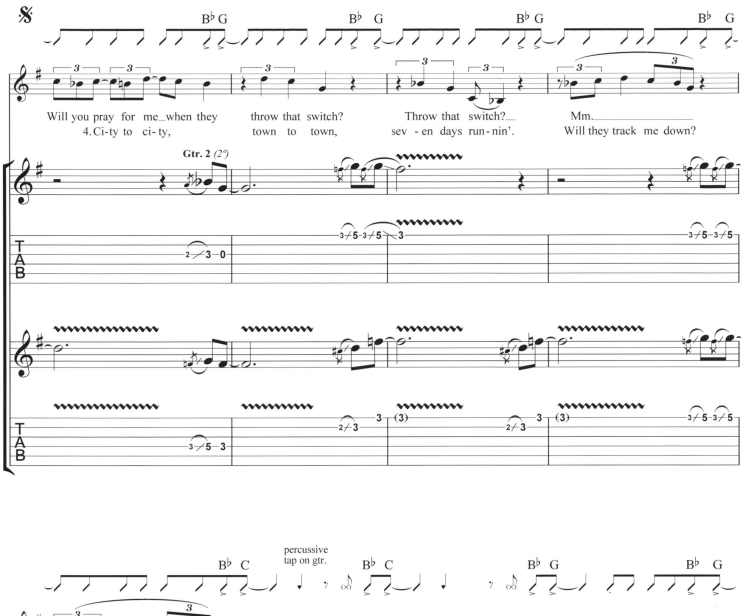

Will you pray for me_when they throw that switch? Throw that switch?__ Mm._____
4.Ci-ty to ci-ty, town to town, sev - en days run-nin'. Will they track me down?

**Gtr. 2** *(2°)*

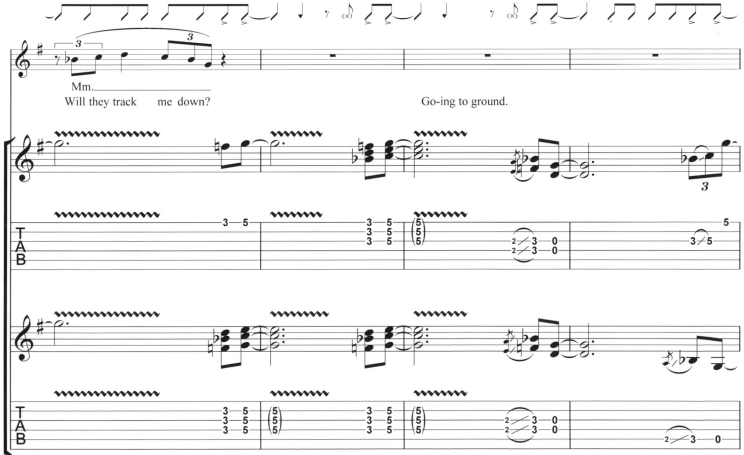

Mm._____ Will they track me down?

Go-ing to ground.

percussive
tap on gtr.

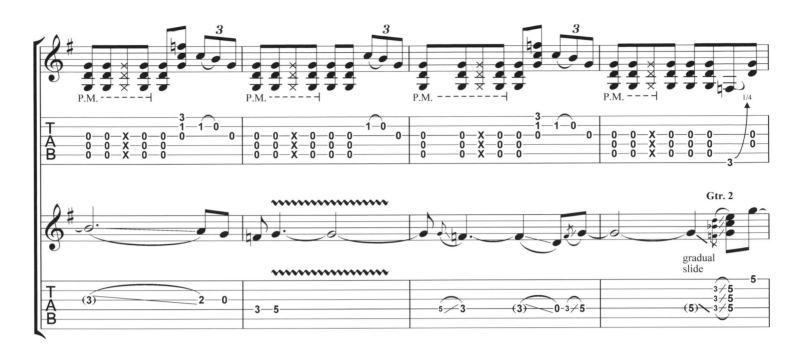

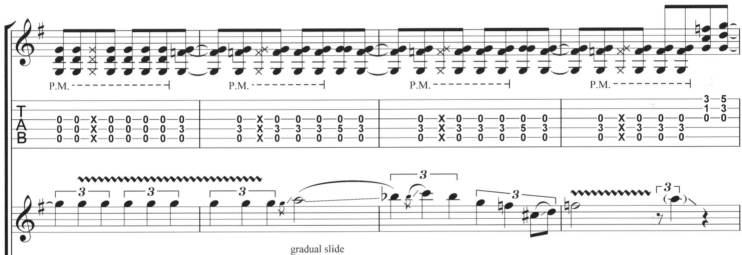

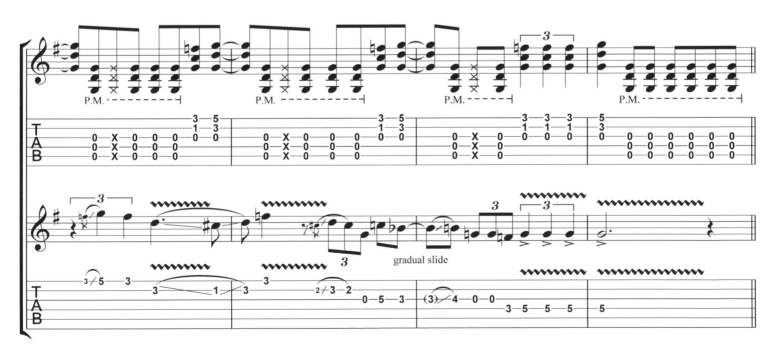

# 20:20 VISION

Words & Music by Rory Gallagher

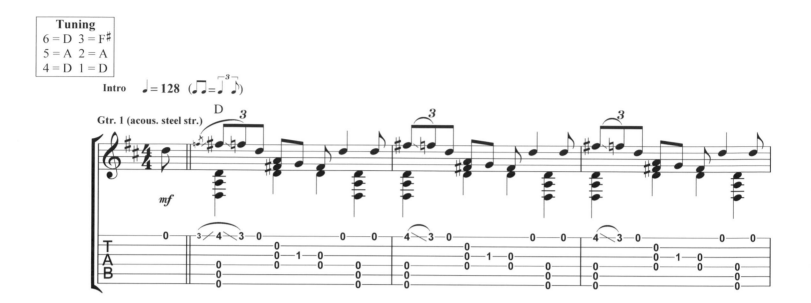

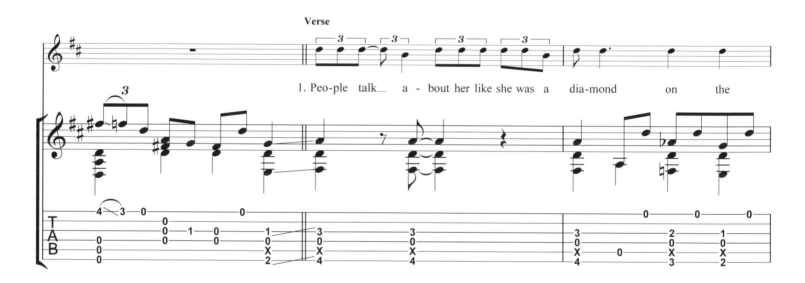

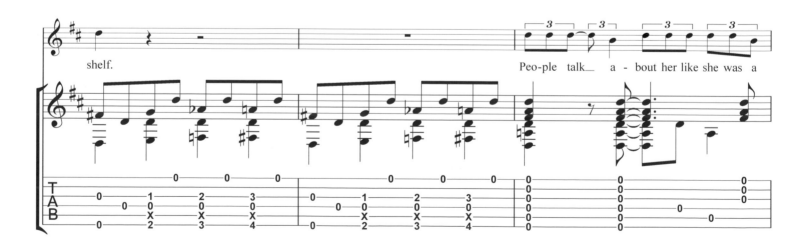

dia-mond      on    the    shelf.                                                        Well, I got

twen-ty twen-ty vi - sion, I can see____ that for____ my - self.____

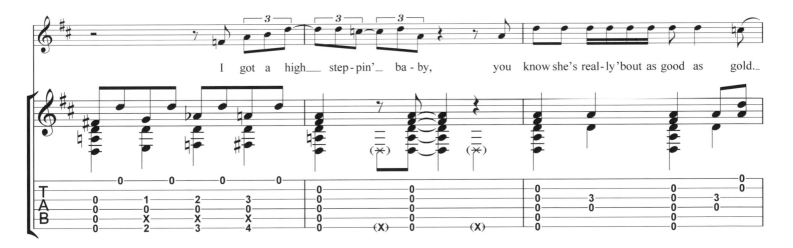

I  got a high____ step-pin'__ ba - by,        you  know she's real-ly 'bout as good as    gold.__

____         I  got a high____ step-pin'__ ba - by,        you

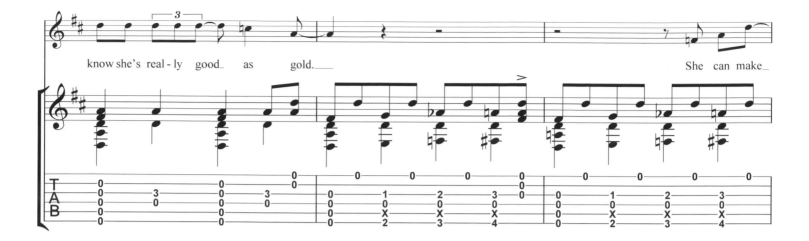

know she's real-ly good_ as_ gold._ She can make_

— my_ grand - pa_ feel like he's six_ years old.

**Chorus**

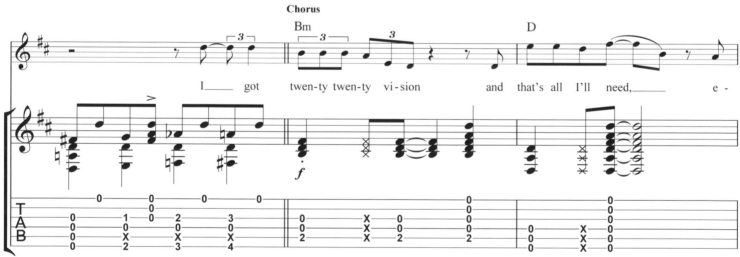

I_ got twen-ty twen-ty vi-sion and that's all I'll need,_ e -

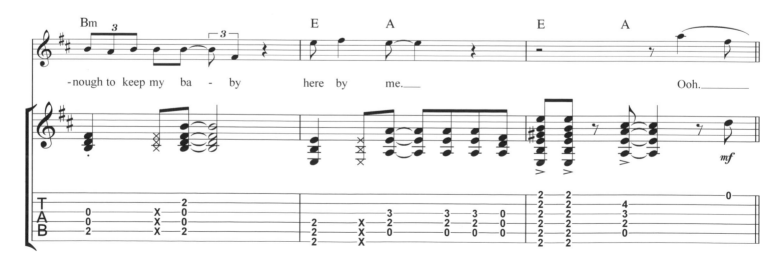

-nough to keep my ba - by here by me._ Ooh._

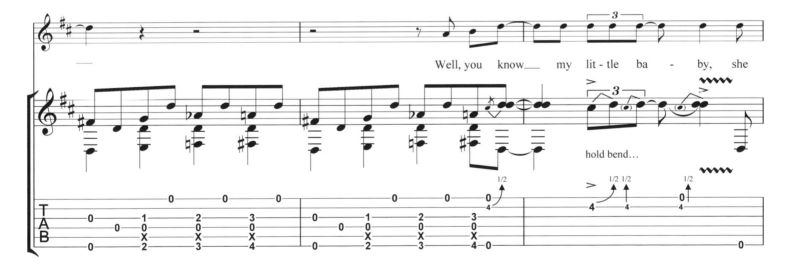

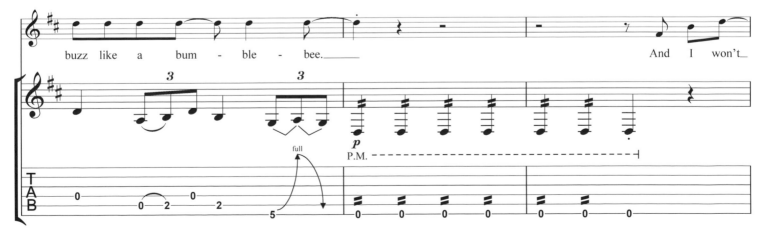

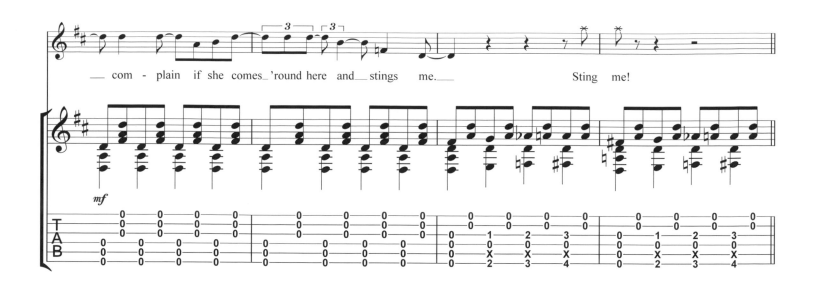

com - plain if she comes 'round here and stings me. ___ Sting me!

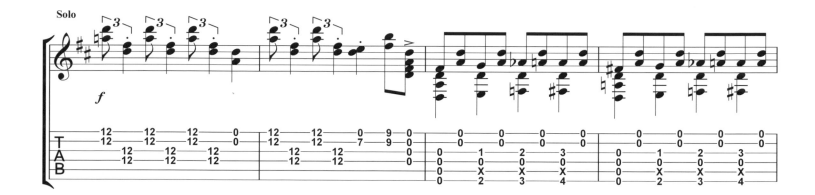

Solo

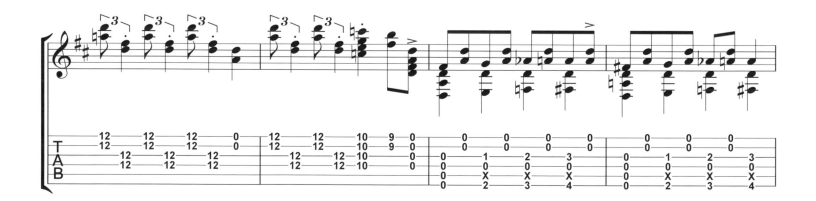

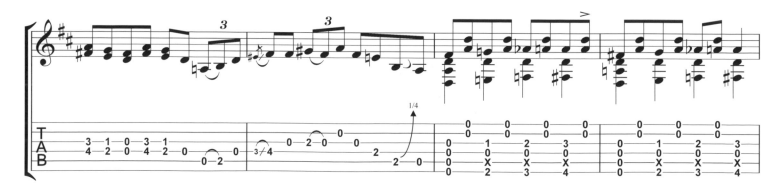

w/harmonica

**Harmonica solo**

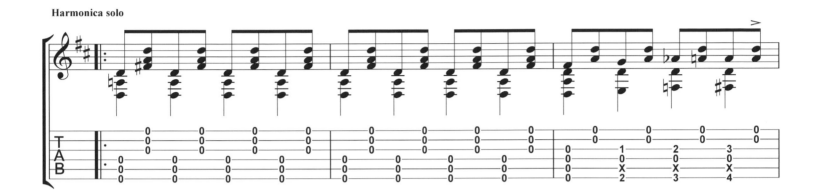

**1.**　　　　　　　　**2.**　　　　　　　**Chorus**

Bm

I got twen-ty twen-ty vi-sion and

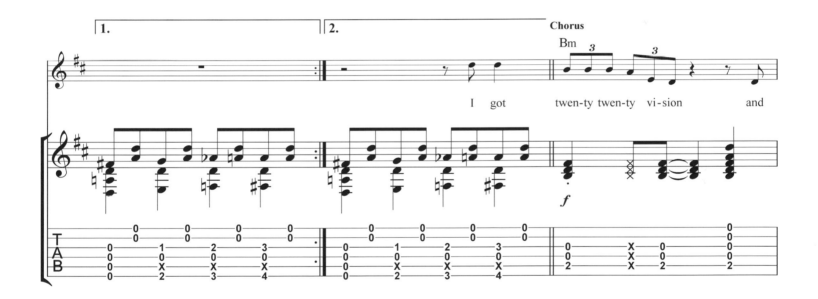

D　　　　　　　　　　　Bm　　　　　　　　　　E　　A

that's all I'll need,＿＿＿ e - nough to keep＿ my ba-by good＿ com-pa - ny.　　Yeah.

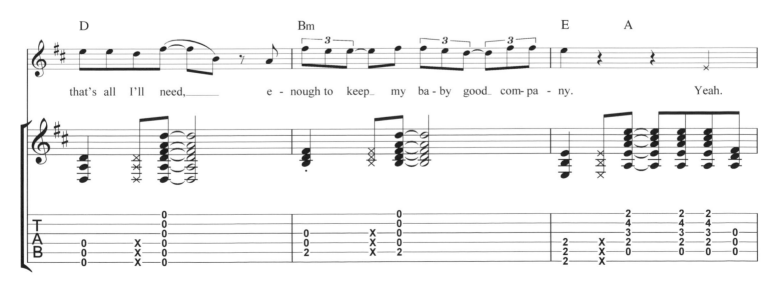

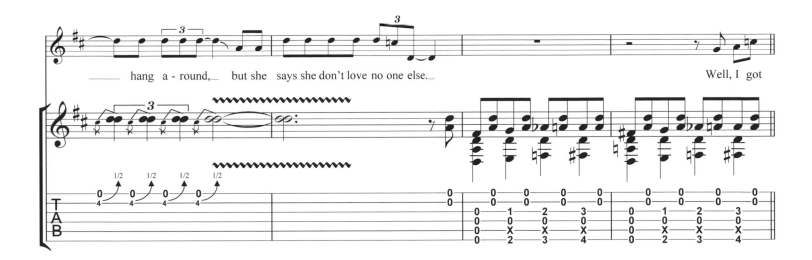

hang a - round, but she says she don't love no one else.       Well, I got

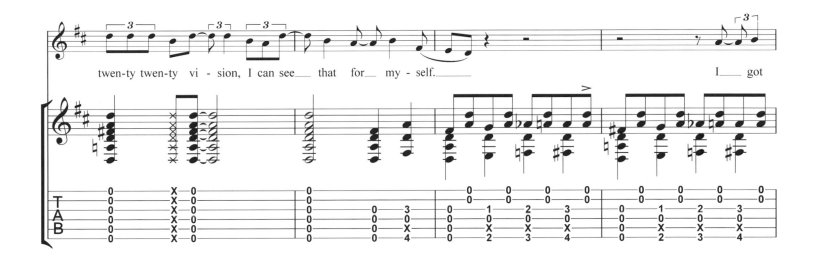

twen-ty twen-ty vi - sion, I can see  that for  my-self.          I  got

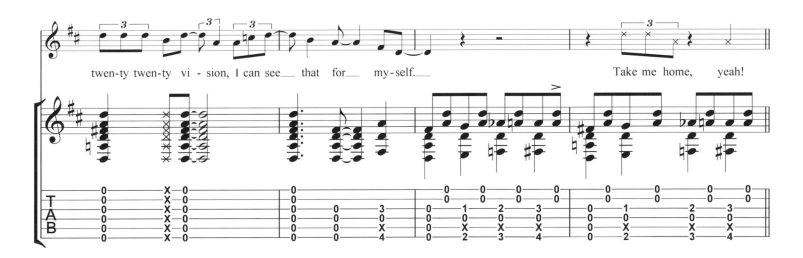

twen-ty twen-ty vi - sion, I can see  that for  my-self.        Take me home,     yeah!

**Piano solo**

*Repeat to fade*

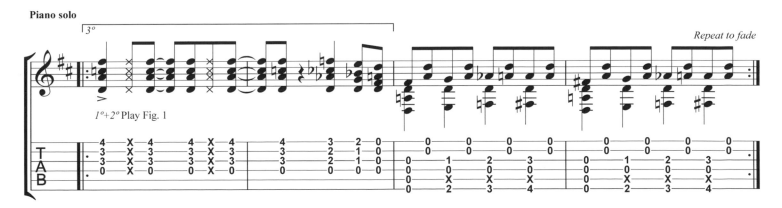

*1º+2º* Play Fig. 1

# WAVE MYSELF GOODBYE

Words & Music by Rory Gallagher

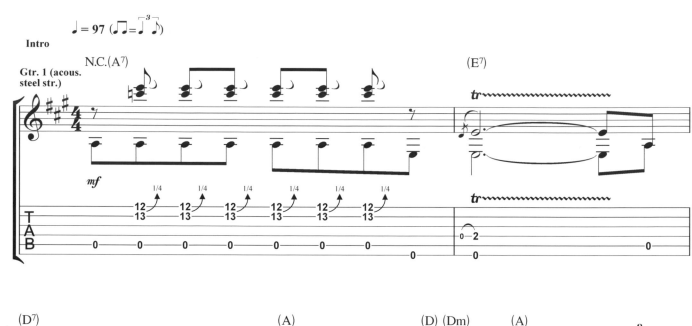

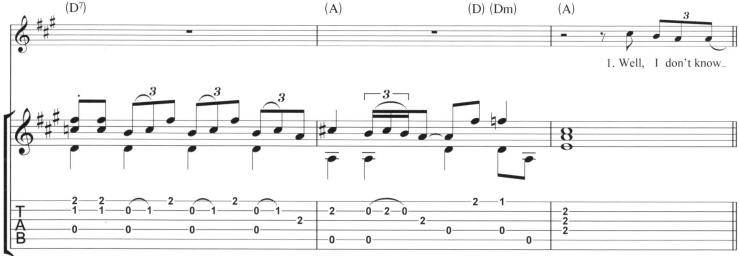

1. Well, I don't know_

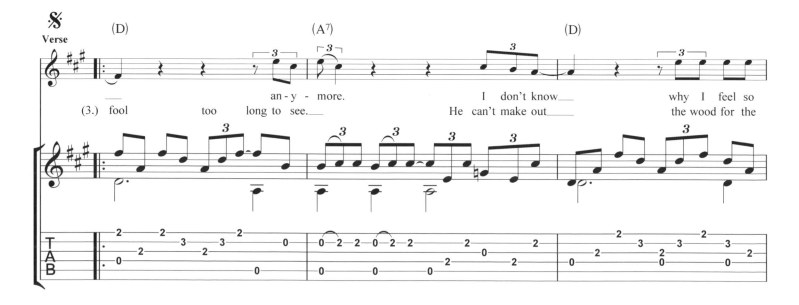

an-y-more.          I don't know_          why I feel so

(3.) fool          too          long to see.___          He can't make out___          the wood for the

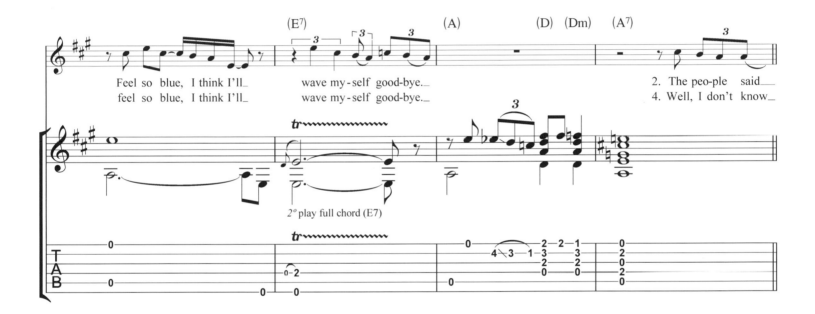

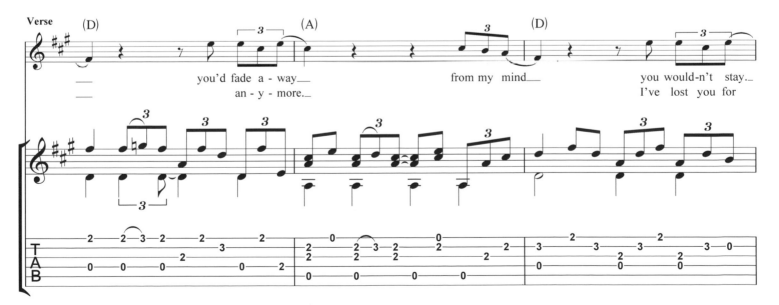

142

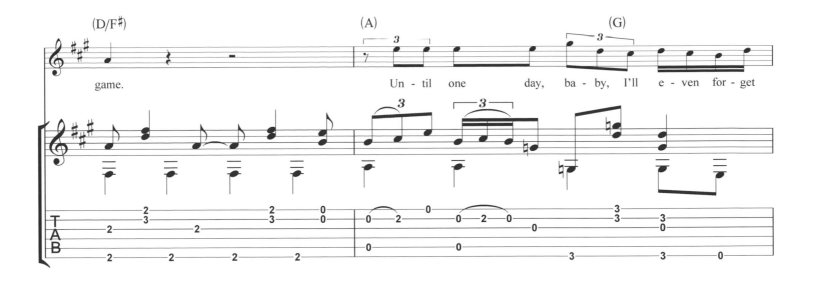

game.    Un - til one    day, ba - by, I'll e - ven for - get

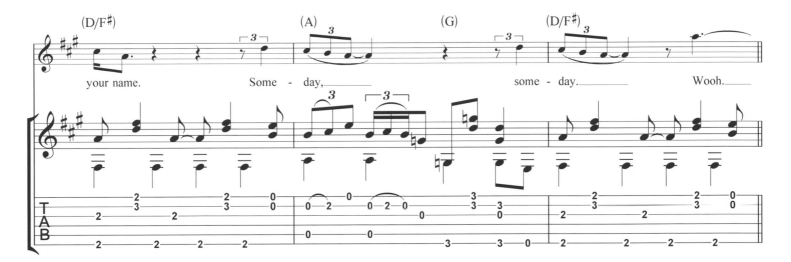

your name.    Some - day,_____    some - day._____    Wooh._____

**Piano solo**

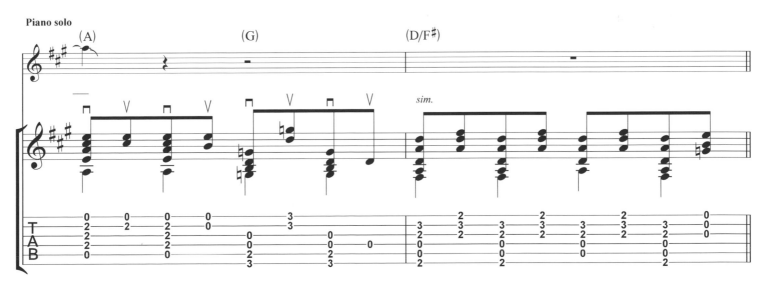

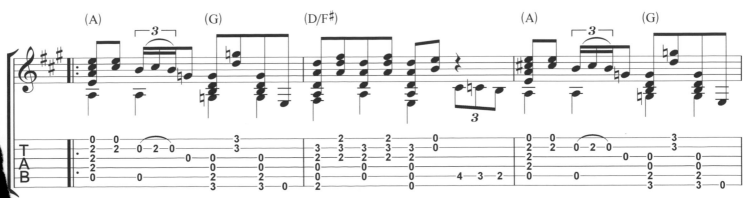

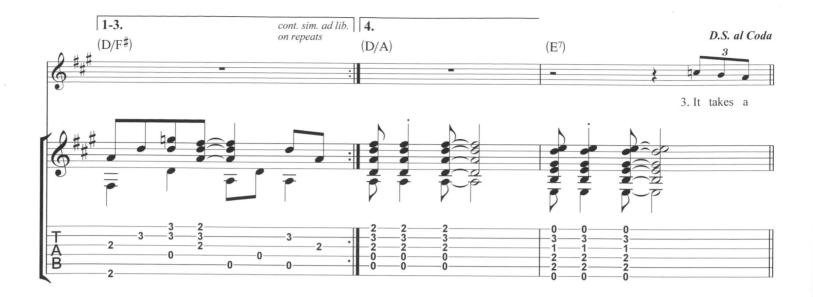

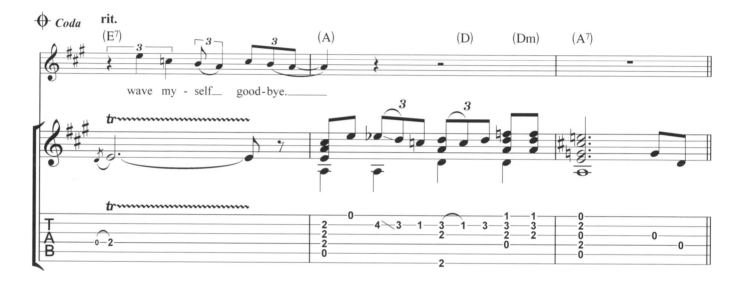

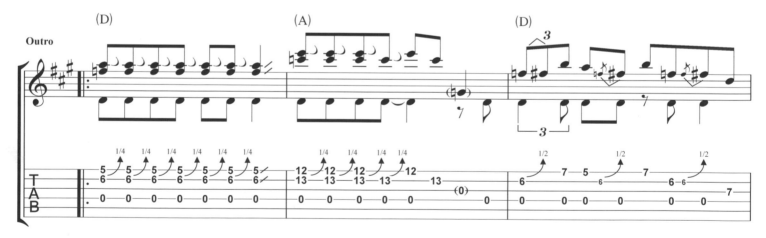